W9-APQ-171

Anthropology Glossary

DEFINING THE FIELD THROUGH ITS TERMS

Second Edition

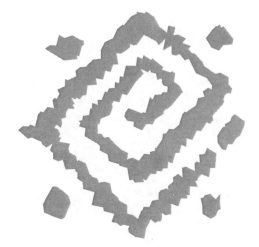

Paul V. McDowell
Santa Barbara City College

Kendall Hunt
publishing company

www.kendallhunt.com
Send all inquiries to:
4050 Westmark Drive
Dubuque, IA 52004-1840

Copyright © 2005, 2009 by Paul V. McDowell

ISBN 978-0-7575-6811-4

Kendall/Hunt Publishing Company has the exclusive rights to reproduce this work,
to prepare derivative works from this work, to publicly distribute this work,
to publicly perform this work and to publicly display this work.

All rights reserved. No part of this publication may be reproduced,
stored in a retrieval system, or transmitted, in any form or by any
means, electronic, mechanical, photocopying, recording, or otherwise,
without the prior written permission of Kendall/Hunt Publishing Company.

Printed in the United States of America
10 9 8 7 6 5 4 3

Contents

Topical Glossary in Anthropology   1

Alphabetical Glossary in Anthropology   57

Kinship Diagrams   107

TOPICAL GLOSSARY IN ANTHROPOLOGY

Chapter 1
Introduction

Anthropology: The *holistic* and comparative study of humankind.

Archaeology: The comparative study primarily of cultural remains of human societies, although the study of fossil hominids (earlier human and humanlike forms) relevant to material culture (e.g., tool making) is also included.

Cultural Anthropology (also known as **sociocultural anthropology** and **ethnology**): The comparative study of human behavior according to the rules, usually implicit, of the society of which individuals are a part.

Culture (E.B. Tylor, founder of anthropology in Great Britain): "That complex whole which includes knowledge, belief, art, law, morals, custom, and any other capabilities and habits acquired by man as a member of society."

Culture (Haviland): The values, beliefs, and perceptions of the world shared by members of a society that they use to interpret experience and generate behavior and that are reflected in their behavior (2002:34). Cultures are learned, symbolic, shared, patterned, and generally adaptive. See text for explanation.

Linguistics: The comparative study of language, primarily as it is spoken.

Physical Anthropology: The comparative study of the biological aspects of humankind of both contemporary population and fossil forms.

Chapter 2
Anthropological Principles

Anthropological Theoretical Orientations

Cross-Cultural Comparison: The comparison of two or more cultures with regard to a certain trait or complex of traits. If any generalization is to hold up for all the peoples of the world, then it must be tested with instances from several cultures.

Cultural Relativism: Cultural relativism refers to the idea that, because all cultures are unique, they can be evaluated only according to their own standards and values. Interpretations range from the **Noble Savage Complex** that sees "primitive" societies as free from the corrupting influences of civilization to an anthropological version of **scientific detachment,** or the open-mindness that is characteristic of scientific inquiry.

Cultural Universalism: The idea that all people, regardless of culture, have many things in common. An imperfect opposite to *cultural relativism,* but without the notion of the superiority of one's culture.

Culture Bound: (adj.) Related to ethnocentrism, but with the interpretation that all phenomena are "screened" through one's own "cultural filters," whether such screening is conscious or not.

Ethical Relativism: Defined as tolerance of practices harmful to the body or psyche of the victims.

Ethnocentrism: The belief in the superiority of one's own culture over all other cultures.

Holism: A fundamental principle in anthropology that aspects of any culture must be viewed in the broadest possible context to understand their interconnections and interdependence. All aspects of a culture are considered, together with their mutual fit.

Research Techniques

Informant: Persons providing information about their culture or (in linguistics) about their language.

Interviews: Research that involves asking *informants* questions about their culture, or asking why people do what they do.

Key Informant: Person upon whom the ethnographer primarily or initially depends for information regarding a culture; often selected for extensive knowledge or important local interpersonal connections.

Observation: Informed watching of the behavior of people within a culture with the aim not only of describing this detail or that, but asking how it fits in with the rest of the culture. It may involve learning the language, and observing how that language structures the reality experienced by the people being studied.

Open-Ended Interviews: Unstructured interviews, generally without detailed questionnaires.

Participant Observation: Observation that involves taking part in the activities of the people under study, and describing the experience of this participation.

Respondent: Person responding to closed-ended interviews; often used in sociology, political science, and other social sciences.

Restudy: Research conducted of a culture previously studied, usually by another anthropologist; the rough anthropological equivalent to *replication.*

Research Methodology

Comprehensiveness: The rule whereby a proposition must be tested by all relevant information and data, by those that not only support the proposition but also those that do not support it.

Falsifiability: The rule whereby a proposition must be so stated that it is rejected if it fails to pass a test (in the laboratory or in the field).

Honesty: The rule whereby a researcher must be prepared to accept the outcome of the test or assessment, whatever that may be.

Hypothesis: A proposition set forth to be tested. Often referred to as "an educated guess."

Logic: The rule whereby a proposition must be both *sound*, that is, be truthful, and *valid*, that is, be based on solid reasoning. A statement can be sound but invalid or be unsound but valid.

Proposition: A statement positing a relationship between two or more things and events. That cultures universally prohibit incest is an example of a proposition (a rather broad one).

Replication: The rule whereby any verified proposition must be subjected to a second test or assessment involving conditions that are identical to the first.

Research Method: The reasoning that leads to the choice among possible research techniques, and the justification for making the choice. Often used interchangeably with *research techniques,* thus creating confusion.

Research Methodology: The principles or research problems that govern the rationale behind a given set of *research methods.*

Research Techniques: Any of several direct ways for gathering information: *observation, participant observation, interview,* technological devices such as videotapes and tape recorders, photographs, written records analysis, and a host of others.

Sound: (adj.) The norm that a proposition be true.

Sufficiency: The rule whereby evidence to support the proposition must be adequate with the following stipulations: (a) the burden of proof rests on the author of the proposition; (b) extraordinary propositions require extraordinary evidence; and (c) evidence based on authority or testimony is never adequate.

Theoretical Orientation: A body of propositions oriented to models that guide research. Examples include culture ecology and functionalism. See under "Anthropological Theory."

Theory: A hypothesis confirmed by laboratory tests, field research, or other means of verification. All theories are *probabilistic:* a theory currently accepted may later be rejected as new evidence becomes available.

Validity: (adj.). The norm that one proposition logically follows from another.

Chapter 3
Human Evolution: Biological and Cultural

Genetics

Allele: One of a pair of *genes* that codes for variations of a specific trait in the organism.

Breeding Population: Within a species, a community of individuals where mates are usually found.

Cell: The smallest unit capable of performing all functions of a living organism.

Chromosomes: Strings of hereditary material, made up of **DNA,** which contain the codes for all physical traits of the organism.

Codominant (Genetics): (adj.) The situation in which, in a *heterozygous* individual, both alleles are expressed in the phenotype.

Cytoplasm: All the material found in a gelatin-like substance between the membrane of the nucleus and the wall of the cell.

DNA: see *Deoxyribonucleic Acid.*

Deleterious Mutation: A *mutation* that renders an organism maladaptive to a given environment. Most mutations are deleterious.

Deoxyribonucleic Acid (DNA): Long double spirals of molecules comprising sugar and phosphate molecules, together with paired bases that link the two strands. Also known as *chromosomes,* DNA contains the codes for all physical traits of the organism.

Diploid: (adj.) Refers to double the number of chromosomes in an organism during *mitosis.*

Dominant (genetics): (adj) The situation in which, in a *heterozygous* individual, only one *allele* is expressed in the *phenotype.*

Gamete: Sex cell, either *sperm* or *ovum.*

Gene Flow: The introduction of new genes to an existing population through migration.

Genes: Segments of **chromosomes** or **DNA** that code for specific traits of the organism.

Genetic Drift: Changes in genetic composition—that is, allele frequency—by chance or random factors in small populations.

Genotype: The genetic composition of the organism.

Haploid: (adj.) Refers to half the pair in the number of chromosomes of an organism in a **gamete.**

Heterozygous: (adj.) Having two unlike **alleles** of a particular **gene.**

Homozygous: (adj) Having two like **alleles** of a particular **gene.**

Meiosis: Division of a gamete into two, each one containing half the chromosomes of somatic cells.

Mitosis: Division of one **somatic cell** into two.

Mutation: An alteration in the genetic material.

Natural Selection: Genetic change in the frequency of certain traits in breeding populations because of differential reproductive success between individuals.

Nucleus: The structure inside the cell that contains the **chromosomes.**

Ovum (pl. ova): Female sex cell; when fertilized it becomes a **zygote.**

Phenotype: The observable and measurable characteristics of an organism.

Recessive (Genetics): (adj.) The situation in which, in a **heterozygous** individual, the gene is not expressed in the phenotype; the trait becomes phenotypic only if the individual is **homozygous** for that trait.

Sickle-Cell Anemia: A severe hemoglobin (red blood cellular) disorder that results from inheriting two copies of a mutant allele characterized by red blood cells assuming a sickle shape; such cells block capillaries, resulting in anemia, heart disease, and ultimately, death.

Somatic Cell: Any cell of the body except the sex cells, or **gametes.**

Sperm: Male sex cell, which fertilizes the **ovum.**

Tay-Sachs Disease: An enzyme deficiency of lipid metabolism inherited through a pair of recessive alleles, causing death in early childhood.

Trait: The physical characteristics of any organism.

Zygote: Fertilized ovum, which develops into an embryo and fetus through mitosis.

Taxonomy

Animalia: Lifeforms of a kingdom that feed on other lifeforms, are incapable of producing their own food, and are motile, or mobile.

Anthropoidea: Monkeys, apes, and humans, but not prosimians, which belong to that *suborder.*

Australopithecines: See under **Hominid Evolution.**

Australopithecus: See under **Hominid Evolution.**

Catarrhini: Old World monkeys, apes, and humans, all with projecting noses and nostrils pointed downward, all which belong to that *infraorder.* This category excludes all New World Monkeys, which have flat noses and therefore categorized as Platyrrhini.

Chordata: Animals with spinal cords. Humans belong to that *phylum.*

Cladistics: Classification system based on order of evolutionary branching based on genetics instead of present similarities and differences.

Class (Taxonomic): A subcategory of *subphylum* (or superclass, as the case may be) which includes **Mammalia.**

Family: A subcategory of *superfamily* (taxonomies vary) that comprises all *hominids* (modern and fossil human forms), *Pongidae* (great apes) and *Hylobatidae* (gibbons, or lesser apes).

Genus: A group of closely related *species.*

Hominidae: A *family* that comprises the *genera* Australopithecus, *Paranthropus,* and **Homo.** Characterized by *bipedalism,* progressively reduced *dentition,* progressively larger and more complex brains, and the capability of fine manipulation with hands.

Hominoids: A *superfamily* comprising apes and humans. Characterized by relative large and complex brains, absence of a tail, and relatively complex social behavior. See text.

Homo: See under **Hominid Evolution.**

Homo erectus: See under **Hominid Evolution.**

Homo habilis: See under **Hominid Evolution.**

Homo heidelbergensis: See under **Hominid Evolution.**

Homo neanderthalensis: See under **Hominid Evolution.**

Homo sapiens: See under **Hominid Evolution.**

Hylobatidae: A *family* that comprises the lesser apes, the gibbons and the siamangs. Includes specialized **brachiation.**

Infraorder: A subcategory of *suborder* that includes Old World monkeys, apes, and humans.

Kingdom: The largest division in the taxonomy of living forms. They include *Plantae* (plants) and *Animalia* (animals), along with three other kingdoms.

Lumpers: Taxonomists who would make broader distinctions between *taxa;* for example, lumpers would place humans and Neanderthals into one *species.*

Mammalia: Animals with internal body temperature regulation, usually with hair or fur, and whose females secrete milk. Humans belong to that *class.*

Nomenclature: Naming system based on taxonomy.

Order: A subcategory of *class* (or subclass, superorder, or other category, depending on lifeforms and taxonomic scheme) which includes *Primata.*

Panidae: In some taxonomies, a *family* that includes chimpanzees, bonobos, and gorillas, but excludes orangutans, who remain the sole members of the family *pongidae.*

Phenetic Taxonomy: Taxonomy based on physical and adaptive traits of a lifeform.

Phylum: A subcategory of *kingdom* that includes *Chordata* or animals with spinal cords.

Plantae: Lifeforms of a *kingdom* that produce their own food by photosynthesis and are incapable of movement, or sessile.

Pongidae: A *family* that comprises the great apes: chimpanzees, bonobos, gorillas, and orangutans. Some taxonomies include orangutans only, whereas the others are classified as *Panidae.*

Primata: Animals with stereoscopic vision, opposable thumbs, relatively large brains, and complex social behaviors and relations. See text for further discussion. Humans belong to that *order.*

Speciation: The process by which new species are developed from earlier ones.

Species: The largest natural population whose members are able to reproduce successfully (i.e., reproduce fertile offspring) but not with members of other species. By that definition, *Homo sapiens* is one species.

Splitters: Taxonomists who make relatively fine distinctions between *taxa;* for example, splitters would place modern humans and Neanderthals into two separate *species.*

Suborder: A subcategory of *order* which includes *Anthropoidea* and Prosimii, or prosimians, such as the lemurs, tarsiers, and loris.

Subphylum: A subcategory of *phylum* that includes *Vertebrata,* or animals whose spinal cord is protected by a hard segmented column made of bone or cartilage.

Superfamily: A subcategory of *infraorder,* which includes apes and humans. Separates *Hominoidea* (apes and humans) from Cercepithecoidea, or old world monkeys.

Taxon (pl. Taxa): Individual category based on a classification system. See *taxonomy.*

Taxonomy: Classification system based on similarities and differences, arranged hierarchically from the general to the specific.

Vertebrata: Animals whose spinal cord is protected by a bony or cartillagenous segmented column. Humans belong to that *subphylum.*

Comparative Anatomy

Angular Gyrus: Area located in the parietal region, whose role it is to integrate multimodal (i.e., sight, sound, touch, taste, and smell) information from the senses.

Arch (Human Foot): The double curvature on the human foot: the longitudinal arch along the foot lengthwise, and the transverse arch across the center of the foot.

Arcuate Fasciculus: Bundle of nerves that connects *Broca's area* and *Wernicke's area.*

Bipedalism: The ability to walk on two feet. The structure of almost the entire skeleton is oriented around this ability.

Brainstem: Part of the brain that is involved with some of the body functions essential to life; breathing and the heartbeat are examples.

Broca's Area: Area in the *left hemisphere* that is involved with the production of spoken language.

Calcaneus: Heel bone of the foot.

Canine Teeth: Jagged teeth immediately behind the *incisors,* which perform piercing functions.

Cerebellum: Part of the brain immediately above the brainstem which regulates all aspects of body movement, including balance and body position.

Cerebrum: Enlarged anterior of the brain that overlies the other parts of the brain, considered to be the seat of conscious mental processes.

Cervical Vertebrae: Neck bones of the *vertebrae.*

Chin: Bony protuberance projecting outward from the mandible that reinforces the two halves of that mandible; a sure indication that the specimen is modern *Homo sapiens*.

Coccyx: Tailbone; the tip of the lower vertebrae.

Corpus Callosium: Nerve fibers connecting the two **hemispheres** of the brain.

Cranium (pl. Crania): The skull or, more specifically, the part of the skull housing the brain; the braincase.

Dental Arcade: The arrangement of teeth on a jaw; the dental arcade of prehuman primates tends to be rectangular, with the back teeth running parallel; that of middle and recent hominids tends to be rounded.

Dental Formula: The number of **incisors, canines, premolars,** and **molars** on one side of the upper and lower jaw. Humans, apes, and Old World monkey's formula is the same: 2.1.2.3 on each side of each jaw; New World monkeys' formula varies from this formula.

Diastema: In non-human primates and early hominids, the gap between the incisors and canine that accommodates the canine of the opposite jaw.

Encephalization: The proportion of brain size relative to other measures, such as body size; also, the tendency of the human biological brain to increase in size.

Femur: Thighbone.

Fibula: Smaller of the two leg bones, located at the rear.

Foramen Magnum: Large hole at base of the human brain through which the **spinal cord** passes.

Frontal Bone: Foremost bone of the **cranium.**

Frontal Lobe: Foremost part of the **cerebral cortex** in the brain which deals with purposive behavior and conceptual thought.

Gluteus Maximus: Large muscle that attaches the **pelvis** to the **femur;** essential for bipedal gait.

Hemisphere: One of two halves of the brain, with one side of the brain controlling the opposite side of the body. The left hemisphere is concerned with language, whereas the right hemisphere is concerned with spatial abilities.

Hyoid Bone: A bone that anchors the tongue; an important indicator of the presence or absence of language among fossil hominids.

Hypoglossal Nerve: The nerve that runs from the brain directly to the tongue; important for speech articulation. The human hypoglossal nerve is three times the thickness of the chimpanzee's hypoglossal nerve and contains more nerve endings.

Ilium: Upper blade of the *pelvis.*

Incisors: Four front teeth on each jaw which perform cutting functions.

Ischium: Lower bone of the *pelvis* toward the back.

Left Hemisphere: Left half of **cerebrum** which controls the right side of the body and also deals more extensively with language production and reception than does the right hemisphere.

Limbic System: Part of the brain that is involved with several basic bodily functions plus such impulses as sexual desire and self-protection through flight or fight.

Lumbar Vertebrae: Segmented bones of the lower *vertebrae;* often associated with back pain among human bipeds.

Mandible: Lower jaw.

Maxilla: Upper jaw.

Metatarsals: Foot bones.

Molars: Three back teeth behind the *premolars* which perform grinding functions.

Nasal Bones: Bones on the face that support the nose.

Nuchal Crest: Area around the base (humans) or back (quadrupeds) of the skull to which neck muscles attach.

Obligate Bipedalism: Bipedalism is forced by the human skeletal structure; examples are arched feet, bowl-shaped *pelvis,* inward angling of the *femur,* and so on.

Occipital Bone: A bone of the **cranium** located in the lower back.

Occipital Condyles: Rounded process on either side of the *foramen magnum* that articulates the skull with the **cervical vertebrae.**

Occipital Lobe: Part of **cerebral cortex** located in the lower back of the brain; responsible for sight.

Parietal Bone: Top and upper side and back bone of the **cranium.**

Parietal Lobe: Top and upper side and back of the **cerebral cortex** which receives sensory information from the body.

Patella: Kneecap.

Pelvis: Hipbone composed of *pubis, ischium,* and *ilium,* plus the fused *sacrum* and *coccyx* in the lower *vertebrae.*

Phalanges: Digits (fingers) on the hands and digits (toes) on the feet.

Postcranial Skeleton: The skeleton below the skull (in humans) or behind the skull (in **quadrupedal** animals).

Power Grip: Grip whereby an individual grasps an object between the palm and the fingers; all primates have this ability.

Precision Grip: Grip whereby an individual holds an object, for example a pen, between the thumb and forefingers, thanks to the opposable thumb.

Premolars: Two back teeth behind each **canine tooth;** perform grinding function.

Pubis: Lower front bone of the **pelvis.**

Quadrupedalism: The ability to walk on four feet.

Radius: Lower arm, which is located thumb side and moves around the **ulna.**

Right Hemisphere: Right half of **cerebrum** which controls the left side of the body and is also involved with spatial abilities.

Sacrum: Fused **vertebrae** forming part of the pelvis.

Sexual Dimorphism: Physical differences between the sexes. Gibbons lack much sexual dimorphism, inasmuch males and females look very much alike and neither is larger than the other; in contrast, gorilla males are much larger than females; humans fall somewhere in between.

Simian Shelf: Among early hominids and nonhuman primates, the bone structure in the inside curve of the mandible that reinforces that mandible.

Supraorbital Torus: Brow ridge among humans and other primates.

Tarsals: Anklebones.

Temporal Bone: A bone of the **cranium** located on either side of the skull near each ear.

Temporal Lobe: Lobes located at either side near the ears which deal with perception and memory. Auditory cortex handles hearing.

Thoracic Vertebrae: Vertebrae located in the back of the rib cage.

Tibia: Larger of the two leg bones, located at front.

Ulna: The lower arm, which is located on the little finger side that rotates and moves the **radius.**

Vertebrae: Segmented backbone.

Wernicke's Area: Area in the **left hemisphere** that is involved with the perception of spoken language.

Hominid Evolution

Australopithecines: Generic category that includes both *Australopithecus* and *Paranthropus.*

Australopithecus: A genus comprising early hominids with bipedalism, lower **cranial capacity,** and no direct evidence of stone tool manufacture and use. Include *Australopithecus afarensis, Australopithecus africanus, Australopithecus garhi,* and others. **Lumpers** would include *Paranthropus* as well.

Homo: Genus characterized by bipedalism, large and complex brains compared to *Australopithecus,* and confirmed ability to make and use tools. See text for other attributes.

Homo erectus: First known *Homo* species to use fire and to make relatively sophisticated stone tools, including the **Acheulean tradition** in Africa and Europe, but not in Asia. See text and **Movius Line.**

Homo habilis: First known *Homo* species with confirmed ability to make and use stone tools, these of the **Oldowan tradition.** See text.

Homo heidelbergensis: Also known as "archaic" *Homo sapiens;* fossil specimens vary widely in apelike characteristics around skull, such as **prognathism.** See text for other attributes.

Homo neanderthalensis: Form of **Homo** with features more robust than *Homo sapiens,* with whom **lumpers** would place in the same species. Associated with **Mousterian tradition.**

Homo sapiens: Modern humans with regional variations in **breeding populations.** Fully bipedal, lacks **prognathism,** pronounced **supraorbital torus,** and **postorbital constriction,** and has most complex brain of all hominid forms. See text for details.

Multiregional or **Continuity Model:** The theory that modern *Homo sapiens* evolved from earlier hominid populations (*Homo erectus, Homo heidelbergensis,* and *Homo neanderthalensis*) throughout the Old World—Africa, Asia, and Europe—at roughly the same time.

Paranthropus: A "robust" form of **Australopithecus** categories as a separate genus by **splitters** but not by **lumpers.** Males characterized by **sagittal crest,** and are larger boned compared to the so-called gracile Australopithecines, but are not larger in body size. Include *Paranthropus robustus* and *Paranthropus boisei.*

Replacement or **Out-of-Africa Model:** The theory that modern *Homo sapiens* evolved into their present form in Africa, then displaced earlier hominid populations throughout the Old World (Europe and Asia).

Tool Traditions

Abbevillian Tradition: A period that included manufacture of asymmetrical handaxes, possibly a transition between the **Oldowan** and **Acheulean traditions.**

Acheulean Tradition: A major archaeological culture of the Lower Paleolithic, whose definitive artifact is a well-crafted, symmetrical handaxe. None was found to the east of the **Movius Line.**

Blade (Tool): A characteristic tool in later periods of the **Paleolithic;** a *flake* whose length is at least twice its width.

Core: Stone from which *flakes* or chips are *flintknapped* with a **hammerstone.** A core may or may not be fashioned into a tool.

Crystalline Stone: Stone containing grain that enables the stone to fracture in a predictable way. Examples are flint, obsidian, chert, agate, and slate.

Flake: Stone chip *flintknapped* from a *core;* flakes may be further fashioned into a tool, or may be tossed aside as a *waste flake* or *debitage.*

Flintknapping: The process of making chipped stone artifacts; the striking of stone with a hard or soft hammer.

Hammerstone: Stone hammer used for knocking *flakes* off a *core.*

Hard Hammer Technique: A *flintknapping* technique for making stone tools by striking one stone, or core, with another stone, or hammer

Levalloisian Tradition: A technique for manufacturing large, thin flakes from a carefully prepared core; first created during the Lower Paleolithic becoming widespread during the Middle Paleolithic.

Mousterian Tradition: A term describing the stone tool assemblages (including notches, burins, denticulate tools, and scrapers) of **Homo neanderthalensis.**

Movius Line: An imaginary line drawn through Central India, east of which no **Acheulean** handaxes have been found. Named after the archaeologist Hallam Movius, who first described this anomaly.

Oldowan Tradition: The name given to pebble tools and flakes during the beginning of the Lower Paleolithic; derived from the Olduvai Gorge in East Africa where large assemblages of these tools were found.

Paleolithic: The first period of human prehistory beginning 2.5 million years ago with the **Oldowan Tradition** and continuing with the **Acheulean, Levalloisian,** and **Mousterian Traditions** up to the **Upper Paleolithic.** The period ended with the domestication of plants and animals, known as the Neolithic, around 10,000 years ago.

Percussion Flaking: A technique for producing stone artifacts by striking or knapping *crystalline stone* with a hard or soft hammer.

Pressure Flaking: A technique for producing stone artifacts by removing *flakes* from a stone core by pressing with a pointed instrument.

Retouching: The shaping or sharpening of a stone artifact through *percussion* or *pressure flaking.*

Soft Hammer Technique: A *flintknapping* technique for making stone tools by striking a stone, or core, using a hammer of antler, wood, or bone rather than stone.

Upper Paleolithic: The period in which tool assemblages became more specialized, the stone tools smaller (microliths), and non-stone materials (bone, ivory, wood) also became commonplace.

Human Breeding Populations

Allen's Rule: A theory predicting that within the same species, the relative size of protruding parts of the body, such as nose and ears, and the relative length of the arms and legs, increases as the average environmental temperature increases.

Eugenics: A *pseudoscience* that attributes differences in behavior or personality characteristics, such as intelligence, to differences in physical characteristics and attempts to breed "pure" **races** on the basis of that belief.

Folk Taxonomy (Racial Categories): The classification of phenomena on the basis of cultural tradition; the concept of *Race* is one example.

Gloger's Rule: A theory arguing that within the same species, there is a tendency for heavily pigmented populations to be located on the equator (given the length of sunlight) and for lighter pigmented populations to be located away from the equator.

Polytypic: (adj.) Refers to species composed of populations that differ with regard to one or more traits.

Pseudoscience: Any belief system making claims to science but lacking scientific *methodology.*

Race: Polytypic variation within a human population that is often based on *folk taxonomy.*

Racism: A *folk taxonomy* that links behavioral attributes, such as intelligence, to *polytypic* differences in human populations.

Sickle Cell Anemia: See under **Genetics.**

Tay-Sachs Disease: See under **Genetics.**

Chapter 4
Anthropological Linguistics:
Descriptive Linguistics

General Terms

Descriptive Linguistics: The description and analysis of the structure and content of an individual language.

Ethnolinguistics: See **Chapter 5.**

Historical Linguistics: See **Chapter 5.**

Signal or Sign: Sound or gesture that has a natural, self-evident meaning.

Sociolinguistics: See **Chapter 5.**

Structural Duality: The quality, distinct in human languages, of two sets of language structure: significant nonmeaningful sounds (**phonemes**) and meaningful arrangements of sounds (**morphemes** and **syntax**).

Symbol: Sound or gesture whose meaning is bestowed to a thing or event that intrinsically has nothing to do with that sound or gesture.

Anatomical Aspects of Articulation

Alveolar Ridge: The gum ridge behind the upper teeth.

Angular Gyrus: See under **Comparative Anatomy, Chapter 3.**

Apex: Tip of the tongue.

Articulate: (verb) To speak; the movement of parts of the speech mechanism in speaking.

Articulators: Parts in the lower part of the mouth involved in articulation. These include the lower lip, lower teeth, tip or **apex** of tongue, **front** or **blade** of tongue, center or **centrum** of tongue, and back or **dorsum** of tongue. See diagram (Fig. 4.1) of text.

Blade (Linguistics): Another term for **front** of tongue.

Body: Another term for **centrum** of tongue.

Broca's Area: See under **Comparative Anatomy, Chapter 3.**

Centrum: Central part of the tongue, sometimes known as the **body.**

Dorsum: Back part of the tongue.

Epiglottis: Thin plate of flexible cartilage that folds back over and protects the glottis (space between vocal cords) during swallowing. Epiglottis and larynx are located in lower position in the respiratory system in humans than in other vertebrates, thereby increasing risk of choking.

Front: (also known as **Blade**): Part of the tongue just behind the apex or tip.

Hard Palate: Roof of the mouth; sometimes also known simply as the **palate.**

Hypoglossal Nerve: The nerve that runs from the brain directly to the tongue; important for speech articulation. The human hypoglossal nerve is three times the thickness of the chimpanzee's and contains more nerve endings.

Labium: Lip, both upper and lower.

Larynx: Voice box in trachea (the main breathing tube in throat) containing vocal cords, which vibrate when voiced utterances are made. The larynx in humans is located in a lower position on the respiratory tract than those of chimpanzees or other nonhuman vertebrates.

Lower Lip: The frontmost of the **Articulators.**

Nasal Cavity: The cavity behind the nose, often used in speech.

Oral cavity: Inside space of the mouth between the lips and the throat.

Palate: Roof of the mouth; also known as the **hard palate** or dome.

Points of Articulation: Parts in the upper part of the mouth involved in articulation, or forming of speech sounds. These include the upper lip (the only movable part), upper teeth, gum or alveolar ridge, hard palate, and soft palate or velum. See diagram.

Positions of Articulation: The positioning of articulators relative to points of articulation to form a given sound of speech.

Soft Palate: Synonym of **velum.**

Tongue: The main **articulators** of the **vocal tract,** divided into the **apex,** the **front** or **blade,** the **centrum** or **body,** and the **dorsum.**

Upper Lip: Frontmost of the **points of articulation;** the only one that moves.

Upper Teeth: One of the *points of articulation.*

Uvula: Small, fleshy membranous tissue hanging at the back of the **velum.**

Velum: Soft area behind the **palate** or roof of the mouth. Sometimes called the **soft palate.**

Vocal Cords: Two cords in **larynx** whose folds, when drawn tight, produce the voice in voiced utterance. More specifically, a set of muscles inside the larynx that may be positioned in various ways to produce a voice or other glottal sounds.

Vocal Tract: The oral cavity, nasal cavity, and pharynx (which contains the **vocal cords** and the **larynx** that houses them.)

Wernicke's Area: See under **Comparative Anatomy, Chapter 3.**

Articulatory Phonetics

Apico-Alveolar Stops: Formed by the closure of the tip or **apex** of the tongue with gum or **alveolar ridge.**

Aspirated Utterance: Those involving strong expulsion of air.

Bilabial Stop: Stop formed by closure between upper and lower lips; full term is **labio-labial stop.**

Consonants: Sounds that are produced with a narrow, partial, or complete closure in the **vocal tract.**

Dorso-Velar Stop: **Stop** formed by closure of back or **dorsum** of tongue with **velum** or soft palate.

Fricative: Consonant produced with a constant airflow through the mouth, accompanied by a continuous audible noise (f- or s-sound, which are subtypes).

Glide: A synonym of **semivowel.**

Labio-Labial Stop: Stop formed by closure between upper and lower lips; short term is **bilabial stop.**

Lateral: Sound made with the sides of the tongue lowered (e.g., l-sound).

Nasals: Any sound resonating in the nasal cavity. Produced by lowering the *velum.*

Phone: Any speech sound in a language. Includes clicks and tone of voice.

Phonetics: Study of production, transmission, and reception of **phones,** or speech sounds.

Semivowels: Sounds produced with an articulation like a vowel but moving quickly to another articulation (e.g., w-sound, y-sound). Also known as *glides.*

Spirant: Synonym of **fricative.**

Stops: Speech sounds formed when an articulator is pressed against a point of articulation to stop air passage momentarily. There are other types as well—laterals and spirants to name two.

Unaspirated Utterance: Those without strong expulsion of air.

Unvoiced or *Voiceless Utterances:* Those in which vocal cords in the larynx are not vibrating.

Voiced Utterances: Utterances that involve vibration of vocal cords in larynx, or voice box.

Vowels: Resonant sounds produced by the shape within the **oral cavity.**

Phonology

Allophones: The speech sound variants of the same phoneme. Example: aspirated [kʰ] in key and teak; unaspirated [k⁻] in ski. Note the two k's never occur in the same speech environment.

Environment (Linguistics): The environment in which a **phone** occurs.

Minimal Pair: Any pair of forms (roughly, words) identical except for one **phone** found in the same position within an otherwise identical **environment** (e.g., [bɪn] and [pɪn] are minimal pairs in English. A minimal pair isolates two **phonemes** because [b] and [p] sound different, therefore are significant and make a difference in the meaning of the two utterances).

Phoneme: As used here, the smallest significant unit of speech in a language. It may consist of one phone or more than one similar phones. A phone affects meaning in an utterance (and so is significant) but is not meaningful in itself. Two phonemes sound different to the speakers of the same language (e.g., the two stops in pin and bin in English.) What matters, therefore, is the contrast between two phones or two clusters of phones.

Phonology: Study of **phonemes.**

Morphology and Syntax

Affix: A **bound morpheme** that modifies the meaning or syntactic subcategory of the **base** in some way.

Allomorph: One of two or more variants of the smallest unit of meaning. Example: differences in suffixes of cats, dogs, and horses, which end, respectively, in -s, -z, and -ez (when pronounced).

Base: The **morpheme** to which an **affix** is added (e.g., *cat* is the base to which the **affix** *-s* is added to form a plural. In this case, the affix is a **suffix.).** Sometimes also known as the root.

Bound Morpheme: A *morpheme* that must be attached to another morpheme (e.g., the plural marker *-s* as in *cats*).

Deep Structure: The structure that all languages share, from which rules of transformation serve to generate the **surface structure** of a specific language.

Form Classes: The parts of speech or categories of words that work the same way in any sentence (e.g., Noun Forms: "I see a _____ [dog, cat, mouse; each is substitutable for the other]"; Verb Forms: "I _____ a cat [see, chase, tackle; again, they are mutually substitutable; this process of substitution is called Frame Substitution]").

Frame Substitution: The process whereby the same *form classes* of noun or verb forms are mutually interchangeable.

Free Morpheme: A morpheme that can stand alone and have meaning (e.g., *cat*).

Generative Grammar: Grammar of a specific language whose rules are generated from the *deep structure* of a *universal language.*

Grammar: The sum total of all rules of **phonology, morphology,** and **syntax** for any language.

Infix: An *affix* that occurs within a root or base.

Lexemes: Content of a language, sometimes referred to as its vocabulary.

Morpheme: The smallest unit of meaning in a language. Morphemes may be free (capable of standing alone) or bound (lacking meaning apart from another morpheme). Thus, the expression *cats* is made up of two morphemes: *cat*, which is a free morpheme, and *-s*, which is a bound morpheme.

Morphology: Study of morphemes and their combinations; in reality there is no hard and fast distinction between morphology and syntax.

Prefix: An *affix* that is attached to the front of a root or *base* (e.g., *pre-* in *prehistoric*).

Suffix: An *affix* that is attached to the end of a root or *base* (e.g., *-s* in *cats*).

Surface Structure: Rules governing the grammar of a specific language.

Syntax: Roughly, rules by which words (more accurately *morphemes*) are arranged to form phrases and sentences.

Universal Grammar: A common set of structures that underlie all languages, according to the linguist Noam Chomsky.

Chapter 5
Anthropological Linguistics:
Language and Culture

Communication: A Cross-Species Comparison

Arbitrariness: The absence of a relationship between an act of communication (speech utterance) and its meaning. Acts of communication with intrinsic meanings are called iconic.

Closed Systems (Linguistics): Communication systems whose elements cannot be combined with others to form a third meaning.

Communication: An act by which one organism triggers another.

Cultural Transmission: Acquisition of an element of communication by learning, and with a propensity to change.

Displacement: Ability to refer to things and events not immediately present.

Iconic: (adj.) Term referring to any expression that cannot be separated from its meaning or context.

Interchangeability: The quality of the communication system such that it can be used by both sender (speaker) and receiver (listener) to send and receive messages.

Nonsense Words: Words whose phonemes can be combined to form new combinations, but which are devoid of content. Sometimes formerly nonsense words do acquire content, such as the expression *blip* ([blɪp]) which lacked meaning until radar was invented.

Open Systems (Linguistics): Communication systems whose elements can be combined with others to create new meanings.

Productivity: The property of communication elements such that they can be combined to form new elements which neither the sender (speaker) nor receiver (listener) has heard/seen before, and yet both understand perfectly.

Signal or Sign: See under **Chapter 4.**

Specialization: Ability to transmit highly complex messages by relatively short expressions or utterances. Language is the most specialized of all communication systems.

Symbol: See under **Chapter 4.**

Kinesics and Paralanguage

Chrometrics: Study of the social perception of time.

Haptics: Study of social touching.

Kinesics: The study and analysis of postures, facial expressions, gestures, and body motions that convey meaning, apart from language.

Paralanguage: The extralinguistic noises that accompany language, such as laughing or sobbing.

Proxemics: The study of personal space.

Vocal Qualifiers: Sound productions of brief duration that modify utterances.

Vocal Segregates: Sound productions that are similar to the sounds of language, but do not appear in sequences that can properly be called words. Examples: *oh oh* to indicate apprehension, or *uh* to fill in spaces while the speaker is searching for the right word or phrase.

Vocalization: Paralinguistic noises that are turned on or off at perceivable and relatively short intervals.

Voice Characterizers: Sound productions (laughing, sobbing, trembling) that individuals speak through.

Voice Qualities: The background characteristics of a speaker's voice.

Language and Culture

Code Switching: The practice of changing from one type of language system or dialect to another. For example, Martin Luther King spoke Afro-American English to a black audience and standard formal English to a white or mixed audience.

Dialects: Varying forms of a language that reflect particular or social classes but that are similar enough to be mutually intelligible—Bargains on the West Coast become Bahgains in Bahston, MA. All dialects have the potential to become separate language in time.

Ethnolinguistics: The study of relations between language and culture.

Gender: See under **Chapter 8.**

Kinship Terminology: See under **Chapter 8.**

Lexicon: The entire vocabulary of any language.

Linguistic Relativity: The proposition that diverse interpretations of reality embodied in language yield demonstrable influences on thought.

Sapif-Whorf Hypothesis: The former name of **Linguistic Relativity,** attributed to Edward Sapir and his student, Benjamin Lee Whorf. This is the proposition that diverse interpretations of reality embodied in language yield demonstrable influences on thought.

Sex: See under **Chapter 8.**

Sociolinguistics: The study of language as related to attributes of society, such as gender differences of expression, social class usage, and others.

Historical Linguistics

Core Vocabulary: Part of glottochronology, the pronouns, lower numerals, and nouns of body parts and natural objects used to reconstruct linguistic commonalities and divergence.

Glottochronology: A technique of dating divergences in branches of language families.

Historical Linguistics: The study in the changes and divergences of language over time.

Language Family: A group of languages that are ultimately descended from a single ancestral family (usually reconstructed from this group of languages).

Linguistic Divergence: The development of different languages from an ancestral language.

Chapter 6
Subsistence Systems: Making a Living

General Concepts

Carrying Capacity: The number of people who can be supported by the available resources at a given level of technology.

Cultural Materialism: A theoretical orientation that focuses on technoenvironmental factors as key determinants in cultural adaptation and evolution.

Economy: See under **Chapter 11.**

Liebig's Law of the Minimum: Related to **carrying capacity,** the statement predicts that population cannot grow beyond the limits of a critical resource in an environment, however plentiful other resources may be. Water in a desert environment is an example.

Subsistence Systems: Technology of food production together with the influence that it bears on a cultures' social and economic organization.

Technology: Tools and other material equipment combined with the knowledge for making and using them.

Types of Subsistence Systems

Affluence Hypothesis: Hypothesis that **foraging** peoples have few needs for which a low-yield technology suffices.

Chinampas: Raised fields constructed from alternate layers of earth and decayed vegetation to form a rich—and relatively dry—platform for the crops.

Complex Foraging: Subtype of **foraging** based on high-yield and/or reliable food sources that enable populations to stay at one location; Northwest Coast Native peoples, who relied on regular salmon runs, are examples.

Edge Hypothesis: Hypothesis on the invention of agriculture that suggests that land use became intensified at the edge of natural hunting and gathering habitats by populations that otherwise might have been forced out of such habitats.

Epiphytic Plants: In tropical regions, plants that anchor themselves in treetops but derive their primary moisture and nutrients from the atmosphere.

Equestrian Hunting: As the term implies, hunting using a domesticated horse or other draft animal. Plains Indians are an example.

Flood Plain Irrigation: Irrigation in which fields are abandoned to flooding during the rainy season and planted when the flood recedes.

Food Collection: Subsistence technology which involves primary reliance on naturally occurring food sources.

Food Production: Subsistence technology which involves primary reliance on domesticated plants, animals, or both.

Foraging or Hunting and Gathering: Dependence primarily or exclusively on hunting, fishing, and gathering. Also known as *food collection* in which food sources are those yielded by nature without human modification of the environment.

Horticulture: Agriculture based on hand tools, such as the hoe or digging stick.

Incomplete Food Production: Food production in which primary reliance is on animal but not plant domestication.

Intensive Cultivation: Cultivation involving high crop yield, usually based on technology ranging from the horse and plow and irrigation to fuel-powered farm machinery such as tractors and threshers. Other definitions include that by Melvin and Carol Ember: "food production that is characterized by the permanent cultivation of fields."

Intensive Horticulture: A variant of high-yield **horticulture** and **intensive cultivation** whereby most or all cultivation is done by hand. *Terrace* cultivation in much of East and Southeast Asia is an example.

Irrigation: Any technique of watering crops by diverting water from its source to the fields.

Laterite: Oxides of minerals in exposed tropical soil, rendering the soil unsuitable for cultivation. The process of conversion to oxides is known as **laterization.**

Marginal Environments: Environments considered too arid, frozen, or moist for **intensive cultivation.**

Natural Habitat Hypothesis: A hypothesis proposing that agriculture emerged where domesticated plants developed at the site of their natural ancestors.

Neolithic Revolution: The domestication of plants, animals or both, which first took place about 10,000 years ago.

Nomadic Pastoralism: The type of **pastoralism** in which entire families seasonally move with their herds.

Oasis Hypothesis: Hypothesis that posits that agriculture emerged where there was water in an increasingly water-scarce environment.

Pastoralism: Subsistence based exclusively or primarily on the domestication of herding animals, such as cattle, horses, or sheep. Usually found in semi-arid grasslands.

Shaduf: In Egypt, a lever with a bucket that was dipped into the Nile. The water was then transferred to a sluice and thence to the field.

Simple Foraging: Subtype of **foraging** based on low-yield hunting-and- gathering technology; often accompanied by nomadism, reliance on sharing.

Slash-and-Burn Cultivation (also known as *swidden farming*)*:* In which cultivation is accomplished by first clearing a site of brush and trees and, later, by burning the slash and planting the garden amid the ashes.

Terraces: Cultivated hillside ridges used to maximize arable land and to capture moisture, often involving **irrigation.**

Transhumant Pastoralism: The type of pastoralism based on a pattern of seasonal migration of herds to different environmental zones; usually only men and boys participate, not entire families.

Chapter 7
Principles of Descent

General

Affines (Affinal Kin): Those kin linked by marriage ties: wife-husband, in-laws.

Consanguines (Consanguineal Kin): Those kin linked by "blood" ties: parent-child (generational) or those of brothers and/or sisters (sibling [s]), or both.

Generational Links: On a kinship chart, ties linking a person of one generation to another person of the next generation.

Reckoning (of Kin): Selective recognition of (usually) biological kin as members of one's own family or other kinship unit (however, nonkin can be "adopted" and so also "reckoned" as kin, such as godparenthood in Latin countries and adoption in Polynesia).

Sibling Link: On a kinship chart, a tie linking a person to his or her sibling.

Types of Descent

Bilateral Descent: The rule by which kin are reckoned through both male and female links equally; distance, that is, degrees of removal, rather than sex of connecting link, is used to differentiate kin.

Double Descent (Shorthand for *Double Unilineal Descent):* A system that affiliates an individual with a group of matrilineal kin for some purposes and with a group of patrilineal kin for other purposes.

Matrilineal Decent: Rule of affiliation with a group of kin through descent links of females only.

Patrilineal Decent: Rule of affiliation with a group of kin through descent links of males only.

Rules of Descent (Descent): Rules that connect individuals with particular sets of kin because of presumed known or presumed common ancestry.

Unilineal Decent: Rule of affiliation with a group of kin through descent links of one sex only.

Chapter 8
Sex and Gender

General Terms

Gender: The elaborations and meanings assigned by cultures to the biological differentiations of the sexes.

Primary Sex Characteristics: Reproductive systems of the two sexes: the penis, testicles, and associated genital parts of men; and the vagina, fallopian tubes, and uterus of women.

Secondary Sex Characteristics: Derived physical characteristics, such as greater size and wedge-like body structure of men and breasts and wider hips of women.

Sex: The physical characteristics of men and women.

Sexual Dimorphism: Differences in size and appearance of males and females of any species, including human; differences are greater in some species than in others.

Human Sexuality

Childhood Familiarity Explanation: The explanation that the **incest tabu** arises from the lack of interest or revulsion of sexual behavior between siblings or other individuals reared together from childhood (such as those on an Israeli kibbutz).

Exogamy: Marriage outside a particular group or category of individuals: family (almost always), lineage or clan (usually), village, or other group. Not to be confused with **incest,** which emphasizes sexual intercourse rather than marriage.

Inbreeding Explanation: The explanation that the **incest tabu** arises from the fear of anomalous characteristics that inbreeding would produce.

Incest Tabu: The prohibition of sexual intercourse between consanguineal kin. Not to be confused with **exogamy,** which emphasizes marriage rather than sexual intercourse.

Primary Incest Tabu: The prohibition of sexual intercourse between consanguineal members of the immediate family, namely between mother and son, father and daughter, and brother and sister.

Secondary Incest Tabu: The prohibition of sexual intercourse between specified consanguineal kin outside the nuclear family, usually within the same lineage, clans, or other kin-based group.

Sexual Competition Explanation: The explanation that the **incest tabu** arises from the fear that sexual competition among primary kin will disrupt family ties because of jealousy.

Gender Relations

Berdaches: Among Plains Indians, men who took on women's dress and tasks.

Compatibility With Child Care Explanation: An explanation for the **gender division of labor** in that women tend to handle tasks that they can interrupt to attend to their children.

Gender Differences: Assumed differences between women and men that are attributed to their sex within a given culture.

Gender Division of Labor: The observed differences of tasks assigned to men and those assigned to women in the world's cultures; the gender-assigned tasks differ from culture to culture.

Gender Roles: Culturally derived expectations that are assigned to men and women on the basis of their sex.

Male Expendability Explanation: An explanation for the **gender division of labor** in that men handle dangerous tasks inasmuch as if many men lose their lives to hunting, quarrying, or warfare, reproduction need not suffer so long as most fertile women have sexual access to men.

Relative Strength Explanation: An explanation for the **gender division of labor** in that men, compared with women, have the strength to carry out more strenuous tasks.

Chapter 9
Marriage and Family Formation

Marriage

Concubines: Women cohabiting with men without being legally married; a common practice among royal or aristocratic males in China, for example.

Divorce: Dissolution of marriage, however defined, according to the norms of the society in which it occurs.

Fraternal Polyandry: Marriage of one woman to two or more men who are brothers.

Genitor: A child's biological father.

Legitimacy (in marriage): Social recognition of offspring of a sexual union so that such offspring has full birthright status in the culture and social status to which they belong.

Levirate: A marriage practice in which a widow marries a brother of her deceased husband (a man, therefore, marries his deceased brother's widow).

Marriage (Composite of Today's Definitions): A union between two persons sanctioned by society that involves culturally approved sexual activity and often involves economic cooperation.

Marriage (Notes and Queries): "A union between a man and a woman such that the children born of the woman are recognized legitimate offspring of both parents." (Notes and Queries, Royal Anthropological Institute) There are numerous other definitions of the concept.

Monogamy: Marriage of one man to one woman.

Nonfraternal Polyandry: Marriage of one woman to two or more men who are not brothers.

Nonsororal Polygyny: Marriage of one man to two or more women who are not sisters.

Pater: A child's social father. Although usually the **genitor** and **pater** are one and the same man, in **matrilineal** societies, the pater may be the child's mother's brother.

Polyandry: Marriage of one woman to two or more men.

Polygamy: Plural marriage; marriage to more than one spouse (male or female) at the same time.

Polygynandry: Marriage in which two or more men marry two or more women at the same time. Also known as **group marriage**; this practice is extremely rare.

Polygyny: Marriage of one man to more than one woman at the same time.

Sambandham: Among the Nayar, the right of a woman to entertain one of several male partners at night; a child born to the woman was legitimated when one of the men paid delivery costs, a small gift to the midwife.

Serial Monogamy: Marriage of one man or woman to several partners over time, but one partner only at a time. Example: Remember Liz Taylor? If not, think tabloid.

Sororal Polygyny: Marriage of one man to two or more women who are sisters to each other.

Sororate: A marriage practice in which a widower marries his deceased wife's sister (a woman, therefore, marries her deceased sister's husband).

Woman Marriage: The marriage of two women among the East African Nuer and Nandi, among others, to legitimate the property held by a barren woman and to provide offspring by her partner. The barren woman is the "female husband" in this arrangement.

Postmarital Residence

Ambilocal Residence: One in which the couple lives with the kin of one or the other; the choice is made situationally (one or the other household has more land, etc.).

Amitilocal Residence: One in which the couple theoretically lives with the wife's father's sister; a theoretical construct, no known example exists.

Avunculocal Residence: One in which the couple lives with or near the husband's mother's brother. Occurs in matrilineal societies.

Duolocal Residence: One in which each of the couple lives with her (his) respective unilineal group; one spouse is regarded as a "guest" in the other's home during visits (this form of postmarital residence is rare).

Matrilocal Residence: One in which the couple lives with or near the wife's kin (also known as *Uxorilocal Residence*).

Matri-Patrilocal Residence (usual meaning): One in which the husband and wife live with the wife's kin, then later shifts to the husband's kin. Usually occurs where **bride labor** is practiced.

Neolocal Residence: One established by the couple anew, separately from the kin of either groom or bride.

Patrilocal Residence: One in which the couple lives with or near the husband's kin (also known as **Virilocal Residence**).

Residence: The household in which a couple resides after marriage. Also known as *postmarital residence.*

Types of Families and Households (or Domestic Groups)

Blended Family: Combined family or couple, each with her and/or his own children from previous marriages.

Consanguine Family: A family comprising related women, their brothers, and the women's offspring. Usually found in association with matrilineal descent.

Extended Family: One made up of three or more generations of consanguineal kin (parents and children), together with their spouses.

Homosexual Household and/or *Family:* Household comprising a homosexual couple's household or family and their children.

Household (Domestic Group): That part of a family that shares a common residence; families and households may be one and the same or they may not be. Households are classified by family type; thus, **Nuclear Family Household, Extended Family Household,** and so on.

Joint (Collateral) Family: One consisting of siblings, their spouses, and their children.

Marriage Types also serve to classify family types: **Polygynous Family, Polyandrous Family,** and **Nuclear Family.**

Matrifocal Families: One made up of a woman and her children; the father is absent.

Nuclear Family: One composed of a man, a woman, and their unmarried children.

Patrifocal Families: One made up of a man and his children; the mother is absent.

Rules of Residence: Applied to extended families, separates family types, so that you can have a **Patrilocal Extended Family,** a **Matrilocal Extended Family,** and so on.

Chapter 10
Descent Groups, Marriage Alliances, and Kinship Terminology

General Terms

Descent Group: A group of kin descended **unilineally** or **ambilineally** from a common ancestor.

Egocentric Groups: Groups centered around an individual or group of individuals.

Sociocentric Groups: Groups of organizations centered around descent from a common ancestor.

Unilineal Descent Groups

Clans: **Unilineal** descent groups whose members reckon descent through assumed, though unknown links *(stipulate)* in the male or female line to a common ancestor. In American usage, also known as **sibs.**

Corporate Group: An organized group of kin who controls an estate, exists in perpetuity as a corporate "person," and maintains a body of rights and obligations that extends to all its members as a unit.

Demonstrated Descent: Tracing of descent through known links to a given ancestor.

Intermediate Lineage: Any of a number of lineages embracing **minimal lineages** but also forming a part of larger lineages to the **maximal** lineage.

Lineages: **Unilineal** descent groups whose members trace descent through known links *(demonstrate)* from the male or female line to a common ancestor.

Matrilineages: Those lineages based on matrilineal descent.

Matrilineal Clans or *Sibs (Matriclans, Matrisibs):* Those clans or sibs organized matrilineally.

Maximal Lineage: The largest **lineage** in a society, which usually comprises smaller lineages.

Minimal Lineage: The smallest **lineage** in a society with larger lineages or **clans.**

Moiety: One of a set of two related maximal unilineal descent groups or units in a social unit (band, village, or other such unit). Derived from the French meaning "half."

Patrilineages: Those lineages based on patrilineal descent.

Patrilineal Clans or *Sibs (Patricians, Patrisibs):* Those clans or sibs organized patrilineally.

Phratry: Group of supposedly related clans or sibs (other than moieties). Several definitions have been proffered.

Segment: One of two or more groups whose internal structure (patrilineal, matrilineal, or ambilineal) is similar.

Segmentation or *Fission:* The splitting of a descent unit or group into two or more new descent units or groups. (NOTE: Some intermarrying lineages may divide into smaller intermarrying lineages, as is the case among the Yanomamo).

Stipulated Descent: Tracing of descent through assumed, though not known, links to a given ancestor.

Bilateral Descent and Descent Groups

Ambilineal, Cognatic, or *Nonunilinear Descent Groups:* Descent groups of bilateral kin who, by selection, demonstrate or stipulate their descent from a common ancestor through a combination of male and female kin.

Ambilineal Descent: A form of bilateral descent in which an individual may opt to affiliate with either the father's or the mother's descent group.

Bilateral Decent: The rule by which kin are reckoned through both male and female links equally; distance, that is, degrees of removal, rather than sex of connecting link, is used to differentiate kin.

Restricted Ambilineal Descent Group or *Restricted Cognatic Descent Group:* Bilateral descent groups in which a restrictive rule determines one's membership; an example is the landowning *kainga* among the Gilbertese.

Unrestricted Ambilineal Descent Group or *Unrestricted Cognatic Descent Group:* Bilateral descent group in which all members of the founding ancestor are members; example is the Gilbertese *oo*.

Egocentric Groups

Bilateral Kindred: A group of kin related to a set of full brothers and sisters.

Kindred: Close kin, either bilaterally or unilaterally reckoned, on whom a given ego (from Latin for "I") can call for assistance or to whom he (she) has other types of kinship orientation. Does not involve descent to an ancestor. Except for full siblings (with same mother and father), the kindred differs for each individual, so that kindreds overlap.

Stock: All the descendants of a person or of a married couple.

Unilateral Kindred: A group of kin in which ego reckons only the father's or the mother's retinue of relatives.

Alliances by Marriage

Bilateral Cross-Cousin Marriage: Marriage of a man to a woman who is either his father's sister's daughter or mother's brother's daughter—and who may, in some societies, be both (as among the Yanomamö).

Bride Labor: Practice whereby the groom works for the bride's family or wider kin before taking his bride to his own place of residence. Often associated with **matri-patrilocal residence** whereby a couple lives with the wife's family before living with the husband's family.

Bridewealth (sometimes also known by the less accurate term **Brideprice):** Payment to the bride's family or larger kin group at the time of the marriage. Known by its Swahili term **lobola** reflecting its widespread practice in East Africa.

Cross-Cousins: Ego's father's sister or mother's brother's child.

Dowry: Transfer of wealth from bride's family or kin to groom or his kin upon marriage. Practiced in societies with intensive cultivation, as in European countries. The practice of the bride's father paying for the wedding is a holdover from this practice.

Endogamy: Marriage within a particular group or category of individuals: within a village, band, **caste,** or other group.

Exogamy: Marriage outside a particular group or category of individuals: family (almost always), lineage or clan (usually), village, or other group. Not to be confused with **incest**, which emphasizes sexual intercourse rather than marriage.

Matrilateral Cross-Cousin: Ego's mother's brother's child.

Matrilateral Cross-Cousin Marriage: Marriage of a man to his mother's brother's daughter.

Matrilateral Parallel Cousin: Ego's mother's sister's child.

Parallel Cousin: Ego's father's brother or mother's sister's child.

Patrilateral Cross-Cousin: Ego's father's sister's child.

Patrilateral Cross-Cousin Marriage: Marriage of a man to his father's sister's daughter.

Patrilateral Parallel Cousin: Ego's father's brother's child.

Patrilateral Parallel Cousin Marriage: Marriage of a man to his father's brother's daughter (characteristic of some nomadic groups in the Middle East).

Kinship Terminology: Principles

Bifurcation: Terminological distinction between relatives on the father's side from relatives on the mother's side.

Classificatory Terms: Kinship terms that refer to a wide range of relatives. Example is *cousin* in English, which covers mother's, brother's, father's, sister's land others' offspring of both sexes.

Collateral Kin: Kin descended from a common ancestor with Ego, but who are not ego's direct ascendants or descendants. Examples are Ego's siblings.

Descriptive Terms: Kinship terms that refer to one or at most two kinds of relatives. Examples are *Father* and *Mother* in English terminology.

Lineal Kin: Kin related in a single line, such as grandfather-father-son (patrilineal in this instance).

Merging: Terminological categorization of relatives on the father's side with those on the mother's side.

Aunt/Uncle and Cousin Terminology

Bifurcate Collateral Terminology: Aunt/uncle terminology which father, mother, father's brother, mother's sister, mother's brother, and father's sisters are all distinguished from each other.

Bifurcate Merging Terminology: Aunt/uncle terminology in which mother's brother and father's sisters are distinguished from father's brother and mother's sister, who are not distinguished from father or mother.

Crow System: A mode of kinship reckoning, associated with matrilineal descent, in which a father's sister and father's sister's daughter are called by the same term, a mother and mother's sister are merged under another term, and a father and father's brother are merged into a third. Parallel cousins are equated with brothers and sisters.

Eskimo System: A mode of kinship reckoning in which mother, father, brother and sister are specifically identified. Mother is distinguished from aunts, father from uncles, and siblings from cousins. All other relatives are terminologically merged (for example parallel cousins are not distinguished from cross-cousins and uncles and aunts on one side of the family are not distinguished from the other side.)

Generational Terminology: Aunt/uncle terminology in which the same term is applied for all kin of the ascending generation except for sex of aunt versus uncle.

Hawaiian System: A mode of kinship reckoning in which all relatives of the same sex and generation are referred to by the same term; aunts are merged terminologically with (assigned the same terms as) mothers, uncles with fathers, and cousins with siblings.

Iroquois System: A mode of kinship reckoning in which father's sister is distinguished from mother and mother's sister, mother's brother is distinguished from father and father's brother, and cross-cousins are distinguished from brothers and sisters and parallel cousins. Parents are classified with the same-sex aunts or uncles, and parallel cousins are classified with brothers and sisters. The Yanomamö reckon their kin by this system.

Lineal Terminology: Aunt/uncle terminology which separates the parents from the aunts and uncles.

Omaha System: A mode of kinship reckoning, associated with patrilineal descent, in which a mother's brother and mother's brother's son are called by the same term, a father and father's brother are merged under another term, and a mother and mother's sister are merged into a third. Parallel cousins are equated with brothers and sisters.

Sudanese System: (also known as *Descriptive System*): A mode of kinship reckoning in which a father, father's brother, and mother's brother are distinguished from one another, as are a mother, mother's sister, and father's sister. Cross and parallel cousins are distinguished from each other as well as from siblings.

Chapter 11
Economic Anthropology

General Principles and Concepts

Economic Anthropology (Formal): The cross-cultural study of human behavior that involves the relationship between ends and scarce means that have alternative uses (from L. M. Robbins definition of "economic science").

Economic Anthropology (Substantive): The study of the production, distribution, and consumption of goods and services. Often confused with *technology,* as reflected in such terms as "a hunting-gathering economy" or "an agricultural economy."

Economic Goods: In economics, goods (and services) that exist in finite supply.

Economize: (verb) To maximize the use of one's assets.

Economy: The study of the provision, distribution, and consumption of goods and services.

Formalism: The perspective in economic anthropology that scarcity is everywhere present, requiring economizing behavior everywhere. Time, if nothing else, is scarce, and there are other goods and services, such as prestige, that are usually finite. In those societies, economic analysis is appropriate. Opposed to *substantivism,* which represented a long and ultimately unresolved debate in economic anthropology.

Free Goods: In economics, the existence of goods in such plentiful supply that economic analysis is not applicable. Usual examples are air (ignoring air quality) and, at one time, water.

Scarcity: The notion in economics that goods and services exist in lesser supply than that wanted by humans. The basic postulate is that human wants (needs usually do not enter into the equation) are infinite and that the means for fulfilling them are finite.

Substantivism: The perspective in economic anthropology that emphasizes cultural relativism in the cross-cultural study and comparison of (primarily) nonindustrial economies. Among the principles are the nonexistence of *scarcity* in many societies, the inapplicability of Western economic models and analyses to non-Western societies, and the embeddedness of economies in the other institutions of non-Western society. Opposed to *formalism* which emphasizes universal scarcity.

Technology: Tools and other material equipment, combined with the knowledge for making and using them.

Property

Capitalism: The private ownership of resources and equipment intended for production.

Commodities: Goods and services produced primarily for sale on the market.

Communalism: Ownership of property by a culture at large, such as the hunting territories of the Southwestern African !Kung and other foraging societies. One variation of this involves communal tenure in which individuals have use rights, or rights of *usufruct.*

Feudalism or *Patrimonialism:* An arrangement whereby a serf provides goods and services to the owner of a landed estate in return for protection and the right to use a portion of the owner's property.

Joint Property: Property owned by a *descent group* or *corporate kin group,* and often referred to as an *estate.*

Private Property: Property owned by an individual or individuals. Tenure is often called fee simple.

Property: An asset that is owned by some entity—community, kin group, individual—as observed by members of a culture.

Usufruct: The right to use and enjoy property belonging to another entity.

Division of Labor

Age Division of Labor: The assignment of tasks based on age. The most demanding tasks are assigned to young to middle-aged adults.

Craft Specialization: Assignment of tasks according to ability and training.

Detail Labor: Labor process in which tasks of a given craft are broken down to their constituent parts, with each part assigned to a worker or team of workers. A defining characteristic of industrial society.

Division of Labor: Assignment of tasks to individuals of certain categories based on some criteria.

Gender Division of Labor: The most common division: the assignment of tasks to individuals on the basis of their gender. Except for warfare and public direction (men) and child care (women), there is wide variation as to which task is assigned to which gender.

Distribution/Exchange

All-Purpose or *Multipurpose Money:* Money used for making payment for all, or almost all, goods and services. U.S. currency is one example.

Balanced Reciprocity: Direct exchange of goods and services of more or less equal value, and where tabs are kept. Classic example: Melanesian Kula Ring.

Barter: The direct exchange of a good or service for another without **money.**

Capital: Goods or services intended for production of further goods and services; claims over such goods and services, such as money, stocks, and bonds.

Capitalist Mode of Production: A system of production under **capitalism** in which goods and services are produced for the market, usually by workers lacking means of production other than their labor. The model is M-C-M', where M means money, C means commodity, and M' means increased amounts of money. The aim is to realize a profit.

Command Economy: Economy in which goods and services are controlled by a state; examples are modern socialist states and possibly the Inca, both of which relied primarily on **redistribution.**

Demand: The willingness and ability to purchase a good or service at a given price.

Distribution of Wealth: The equal or differential control or ownership of assets, such as land, productive capital, money and other claims to wealth, and others. *See also* **Stratified Society** *and* **Social Class.**

Domestic Mode of Production: Production oriented primarily for the household; production ceases when the needs of the household are met. The model of exchange is C-M-C, where the householder produces a good or service for sale to obtain another good or service the householder cannot produce.

Exchange: The act of giving or taking a good or service in return for another. Sometimes used interchangeably with *Transaction,* whose connotation is within the context of modern business.

Generalized Reciprocity: Altruistic transaction at which gifts are freely given without keeping accounts. This includes pooling of resources within families.

Hostile Symbiosis: The mutual dependence of two or more parties who are in conflict with each other.

Market Exchange: Exchange of goods or services, either directly (barter) or indirectly with money (prices), by laws of supply and demand. Classic example: Regional markets in Guatemala, Mexico, and other highland Latin American Indian peasants.

Mauss's Theory of Exchange Obligations: *Obligation to give:* in order to extend social ties to other groups; *obligation to receive:* inasmuch refusal represents a rejection of offer of friendship as well; and *obligation to repay:* inasmuch as failure to do so places receiver in status of beggar to the giver.

Money: Any object used to make payment for goods and services. May also be used to measure value of goods and services and as a store for wealth. Often, the material used in the object may lack intrinsic value. Shells in many societies are one example; paper money is an example in Western countries.

Negative Reciprocity: The attempt to get something for nothing, or for something of lesser value. Ranges from bargaining or haggling to less sociable forms such as theft or other varieties of seizure.

Peasants: See under **Chapters 12 and 13.**

Potlatch: A feast among most Northwest Coast Indians held to observe a major event, such as the installation of a new chief.

Reciprocity: Direct exchange of goods and services.

Redistribution: The means by which goods and services (or claims thereof, such as money) are collected by some central agency (chief, monarch, or modern government) and redistributed in the form of some benefit(s) to the people at large. Classic example: Potlatch and other feasts among Northwest Coast Peoples, such as the Nootka and the Kwakiutl.

Rotating Markets: Markets that change location, usually from day to day during a week.

Silent Trade: The exchange of goods and services between partners who are usually in conflict with each other but each of whom has what the other needs or wants.

Solar Markets: Markets located at a central location, usually a town or city, within a region.

Special-Purpose Money: Money used for exchanging special classes of objects; *kula* valuables (white armshell and red necklace) among the Trobriand Islanders are examples. Tokens for bus transit are another.

Supply: The willingness and ability to sell a good or service at a given price.

Tributary Mode of Production: An arrangement whereby elite extract goods in kind or labor from **peasants.**

Chapters 12 and 13
Political and Legal Anthropology Among Egalitarian, Ranked, and Stratified Societies

General Concepts

Authority: In asymmetrical political relations, the process of security compliance by persuasion. Examples range from headman leadership in tribal societies to political campaigns in modern society. Sometimes associated with *cultural control*, or control through a set of shared values and beliefs internalized by members of a culture.

Consensus: The decision-making process based on the consent of all present before embarking on a course of action.

Ideal types: A deliberately simplified and abstract representation of a society or its parts to demonstrate how that society or its parts work.

Legitimacy (In political science and political anthropology): The justification cited for a given political structure, for the right to rule, and the limitations of the exercise of political power.

Negative Sanctions: Punishment for noncompliance, ranging from reprimands and fines to imprisonment to the death sentence.

Political Anthropology: The cross-cultural comparative study of social control, whether informal or formal; includes political organization, formal or not, and law, formal or customary.

Positive Sanctions: Rewards for compliance, such as recognition or monetary rewards.

Power: In asymmetrical political relations, the process of securing compliance by force. Classic examples: concentration camps in Nazi Germany or the Soviet Union or the so-called supermax prisons in the United States, such as the Pelican Bay correctional facility in California. Some anthropologists would see this as the defining characteristic of *social control,* or control over groups through overt coercion.

Sanctions: Reinforcements for a given rule or law.

Sociocultural Level of Integration: The levels of organization in cultures from the local (family or **band**) to the **state** to the global levels; some societies end at the band levels; others add additional layers of organizations.

Territory: The land occupied by a polity (**band, tribe, chiefdom,** or **state**) that is enclosed by boundaries that mark it off from other political entities; they tend to be more clearly defined at the chiefdom and state levels of integration than at the band or even tribal levels of integration.

Integrative Groups: Common Features

Achievement: Assignment to a category based on the person's own efforts, such as an occupational association or union, political party, or interest group such as the Benevolent League of Terminators.

Ascription: Assignment to a social category at birth, such as gender or, as time goes on, by age.

Involuntary Recruitment: Rule whereby one is forced to join an organization, such as the military through the draft.

Universal Ascription: Assignment to any category that affects everyone in all cultures, such as age or gender.

Variable Ascription: Assignment of categories found in only some, but not all, cultures, such as ethnic or regional associations.

Voluntary Recruitment: Rule allowing one to choose to join an association or not.

Kin-Based Integrative Groups

Bilateral Cross-Cousin Marriage: See under **Chapter 10.**

Complementary Opposition: A characteristic of **segmentary lineages** in which kinship groups of equal scope may become allies or opponents, depending on the issue at hand.

Local-Genealogical Segmentation: A characteristic of **segmentary lineages** in which closer lineages also dwell more closely with each other, serving as a physical reminder of their genealogy.

Matrilateral Cross-Cousin Marriage: See under **Chapter 10.**

Patrilateral Parallel Cousin Marriage: Marriage of a man to his father's brother's daughter, designed to keep the assets, such as sheep or horses, within the lineage; frequently practiced in the Middle East.

Segmentary Lineages: A social organization based on local lineages unified by an ever-larger set of lineages that are unified by one maximal lineage. Occurrence is rare, and has been described for the Nuer of Ethiopia and the Sudan, the Tiv of Nigeria, and the Rwala Bedouin of the Middle East.

Nonkin-Based Integrative Groups

Age Grades: Among East African societies, of which Tiriki of Kenya stand as an example, fixed 15-year categories (boys; warriors; elder warriors; judicial elders; ritual elders; and 2 categories of retired and deceased men). Refers to fixed age categories in any society, but East African societies serve as classical examples.

Age Sets: Again as illustrated by the Tiriki of Kenya, movable categories of men who change age grades every fifteen years. Any society with movable age categories, of which East African societies serve as classical examples.

Common-Interest Associations: Associations based on interests other than age, gender, kinship, or territory; resulting from the act of joining.

Ethnic Preservation Societies: Often associated with cultural change, societies seeking to preserve indigenous traditions, such as the Tribal Unions of West Africa, the Mayan associations in Guatemala, and the several Native American associations.

Gender Segregation: Any society in which women and men conduct activities separately; may include residential segregation, as among the Mundurucu of Amazonia or many New Guinea societies.

Longhouses (Iroquois): Houses in which female members of matrilineages and matrilineal clans form the core residents; consanguineal and affinal males are considered "guests."

Men's Houses: In most New Guinea societies, men live together in a common dwelling, handling all the warrior arts, hunting, the dances, and more mundane tasks, such as house repair, clearing gardens, and negotiating pig transactions. Boys move in men's houses at age five or six. Institutionalized homosexuality is often attributed to cohabitation in such residences.

Poro Secret Societies: Secret societies in West Africa Mande-speaking peoples in which all men were **involuntarily recruited** for sacred and secular functions in each **chiefdom** of that linguistic group.

Sande Secret Societies: Secret societies in West Africa Mande-speaking peoples in which all women were **involuntarily recruited** for sacred and secular functions in each **chiefdom** of that linguistic group; women often initiated legal proceedings.

Secret Societies: Societies whose secrets are known only to initiates, often associated with supernatural beliefs, such as the Katchina associations among the Hopi of the U.S. Southwest and the ritual societies among the Kwakiutl of the Northwest Coast.

Sodalities: Groups that cut across kin-based ties, such as **age grades and age sets** in East Africa, **men's houses** in New Guinea, and **secret societies** in West Africa and indigenous North America.

Ranked and Stratified Societies

Brahmin: Priestly **caste,** the topmost of the hierarchy of Indian castes.

Burakumin: A Japanese **caste** considered inferior to all other Japanese; like the Indian **Dalits** they engage in "unclean" occupations such as leatherworking and are isolated in ghettos.

Caste: A social class, within a system of stratification, to which membership is determined by birth and in which the individual remains for life. By definition, such groups are *endogamous.* Indian is best known for its caste system, but Japan also discriminates against *Burakumin* (Japan's "untouchables") and the physically different Ainu.

Closed-Class Society: A society in which **social mobility** is rare or nonexistent.

Conical Clan: Clan whose constituent lineages are ranked by closeness to the chief lineage, one maintained by lines of eldest sons to the presumed ancestor.

Dalit: A member of an "untouchable" **caste** in India who is thought to pollute members of other (**varna**) castes by his or her presence, and pursues occupations considered "polluting," such as leatherworking. The term *Harijan* also applied to this caste.

Diaspora: The scattering of peoples of one ethnicity throughout a wide geographical area, even across the globe. Jews are a classic example, but blacks, Armenians, and overseas Chinese are other examples.

Ethnic Discrimination: Discrimination exercised against specific ethnic groups. Example: In the Mexican state of Chiapas and in Guatemala, Ladinos (who may be biological Indians themselves) discriminate against Indians for their cultural practices rather than their physical characteristics.

Jajmani: An **ascribed** relationship in which a *jajman* provides a good or service to his *kamin* or client; the jajman is born into his occupation and his kamin is his client by birth.

Jati: Any of hundreds of occupational subcastes in India.

Kshatriya: The warrior **caste** in India that includes soldiers and other military personnel, coupled with police and its equivalent.

Nation: Usually geographically contiguous populations sharing a single ethnicity and language; they include stateless nations, such as the Kurds in Turkey, Syria, Iraq, and Iran. Nations without territories are known as *diasporas.*

Nation State: A nation that is governed by its own *state*, rather than the state of another ethnic group or *nation.* Nations without territories are known as *diasporas.*

Open-Class Society: A society in which **social mobility** often occurs.

Peasantization: See under **Chapter 16.**

Proletarianization: See under **Chapter 16.**

Racial Discrimination: The differentiation of groups by physical characteristics and the discrimination exercised against those of the less-powerful group. They include blacks in U.S. society and in apartheid South Africa.

Ranked Societies: Societies in which there are fewer valued status positions than there are persons capable of filling them (Fried 1967).

Rivalry Potlatches: **Potlatches** (see **Chapter 11**) characterized by competitive gift giving by rival pretenders to a chieftainship.

Social Class: A generic term referring to social categories among all societies, from **egalitarian** to **ranked** to **stratified;** they may include subtypes of **gender,** occupation, and social stratum.

Social Mobility: The ability for an individual to move from one social class to another.

Stratified Societies: Ranked societies in which an elite minority controls the strategic resources that sustain life (Fried 1967).

Sudra: The peasant **caste** in India that includes all menial workers.

Vaishya: The craftsman and merchant **caste** in India.

Varna: One of four "pure" castes in India, namely the *Brahmin* (priests), *Kshatriya,* (warriors), *Vaishyas* (artisans), and *Sudras* (peasants).

Sociopolitical Systems

Band: A small nomadic group (averaging around 50), comprising several households, that either lack headmen or includes headmen lacking power and whose influence is derived from persuasion.

Big Man: In New Guinea, a man with influence who mobilizes and manipulates wealth on behalf of his group to sponsor major feasts that enhance his prestige relative to other big men.

Chiefdom: A ranked society with a head whose office is permanent and involves a rule of succession.

Circumscription: The hemming in of a society by geographical barriers, such as mountains, large bodies of water, or desert, such that few options are open to the subjects of a **state** thereby allowing its formation and persistence.

Egalitarian Societies: Societies in which there are as many valued status positions as there are persons capable of filling them (Fried 1967); the **big man** complex in New Guinea is one example.

Peasant: A primary producer, usually an agrarian, who is subjected via asymmetrical ties to a state which exercises domain over his assets for which, according to Eric Wolf (1966), he must provide for a fund of rent. Most definitions emphasize linkages between local and supralocal society, usually a state, as reflected in Kroeber's seminal definition of peasants as "part societies with part cultures."

Pristine States: **States** that theoretically arise in the absence of other states.

Redistribution: See under **Chapter 11.**

Reverse Dominance: The power a group exercises over an individual who tries to assert power over them; means range from ridicule to homicide.

Secondary States: **States** that arise among, and under the influence of, other states.

State: A society with a head whose power is derived from the monopoly of the exercise of legitimate force. Derivative institutions include an administrative hierarchy, delegation of force among police and military institutions, and codified law.

Tribe: A segmentary society with two or more lineages, clans, or other social groups bound together by marriage, pantribal sodalities, such as age grades and sets, more inclusive lineages or clans, or some other unifying factor.

Law and Sociopolitical Systems

Adjudication: Mediation in which the neutral party makes the final decision. Usually associated with a chiefdom or state society.

Codified Law: Written or at least carefully stated law that defines civil breaches and crimes and that specifies the remedies—lawsuit settlements or punishments—for each.

Law: Rules that prescribe individual behavior and means of social control ranging from informal sanctions ("customary") to formal, codified rules of conduct and remedies for violation of such rules. Includes mechanisms for conflict resolution.

Leopard Skin Chiefs: Among the pastoral Nuer of Ethiopia and the Sudan, a mediator charged with the task of resolving conflict between two or more parties (families, lineages). They lack the power to force an agreement between the parties and the power to enforce any agreements that are made.

Mediation: The means of resolving conflict through **negotiation,** involving a neutral third party, of which a **leopard skin chief** is an example.

Negotiation: Conflict resolution or agreement through direct talks to reach a compromise or a mutually satisfactory agreement.

Oath: Act of calling on a deity to bear witness to the truth of what one says in a formal or informal judicial proceeding; the oath in court is a holdover from this practice.

Ordeal: A means used to determine guilt or innocence by submitting the accused to dangerous, painful, or risky tests believed to be under supernatural control.

Restitution: The process, whether in customary or formal law, in which a breach is corrected by repaying the injured party for its loss. Restitution is the primary means of conflict resolution in most non-Western societies.

Retribution: The process, whether in customary or formal law, in which a breach is corrected through punitive means. Retribution is the primary means of conflict resolution in state societies, but it can manifest itself in non-Western societies through blood revenge.

Ritual Apology: A formal apology by the offender to the victim; often accompanied by a reparation gift of value, such as cattle.

Warfare

Feud: A state of recurring hostilities between families, lineages, or other kin groups, usually the product of revenge and counter-revenge killings; among the Dani of Western New Guinea (Irian Jaya), revenge is obligatory, enforced by one's ancestral spirits.

Raid: A short-term use of physical force that is planned and organized to achieve a limited objective, such as cattle or horse theft.

War: Armed combat between human groups comprising separate territorial entities or political communities; at the **state level of integration,** war tends to be systematically planned and implemented; it is likely to involve civilians as well as the combatants, and incorporate progressively higher levels of technology.

Chapter 14
Psychological Anthropology

General Concepts

Behavior: Person's expression of an outward manifestation of the first three elements of personality (**perception, cognition,** and **emotion**).

Behavioral Environment: The world of objects other than self; mediated symbolically through language.

Cognition: Thought processes involved in interpreting one's **perception** of the world.

Core Values: Those values held highest within a given culture.

Emotions: One's affective response to, or feelings about, **perception** or **cognition** of a given situation.

Perception: Sensory input through vision, hearing, touch, smell, and taste.

Personality: The distinctive way a person thinks, feels, and behaves. The components include *perception*, or how one perceives reality through the five senses; *cognition*, or how one interprets this reality; *emotion*, or how one feels or thinks about that reality; and *behavior*, or how one responds to that reality.

Self-awareness: The ability to identify oneself as an object, to react to oneself, and to appraise oneself.

Enculturation

Cognitive Development: The phases of acquiring cognitive abilities in the Piagetan **sensorimotor phase, preoperational phase, concrete-operational phase,** and the **formal-operational phase.**

Concrete-Operational Phase: Age (7–11 years) at which children begin to connect events in terms of cause and effect, and they begin to manipulate symbols in a more nuanced way.

Critical Period of Language Acquisition: Period of time between birth and puberty in which language acquisition must take place, according to the linguist Noam Chomsky.

Dependence Training: Child-rearing practices that foster compliance with the performance of assigned tasks and dependence on the domestic group, rather than reliance on oneself.

Formal-Operational Phase: Age (12 years and on) at which children develop the capacity to think for themselves, and to think of themselves and the world in highly abstract terms.

Freudian Phases of Personality Development: States of development entail the oral, anal, and Oedipal/Elektra stages. Largely discredited, this model is still used by many anthropologists and psychologists alike.

Generative Grammar: See under **Chapter 4.**

Independence Training: Child-rearing practices that promote independence, self-reliance, and personal achievement on the part of the child.

Language Acquisition: Learning a language from infancy to early childhood.

Personality Formation: Child-rearing practices that foster compliance to the performance of assigned tasks and dependence on the domestic group, rather than reliance on oneself.

Preoperational Phase: Phase (2–6 years) in which symbols, including language, are first used.

Rites of Passage: Rituals marking important phases in the life of an individual, in which he or she ritually leaves one status (usually childhood) and enters another (adulthood).

Sensimotor Phase: Phase in which the infant (birth to 2 years) explores the world through touching, sucking, listening, and other sensory modes.

Universal Grammar: See under **Chapter 4.**

Theories of Personality

Color Cognition: Studies claiming that cultures categorize colors in similar ways depending on industrial development, from two basic colors among foragers to eleven among industrialized peoples.

Cultural Configuration: A hypothesis first advanced by Ruth Benedict that a culture is a "personality writ large," whereby a culture represents the sum total of the personality of the people who compose it; precursor of **modal personalities** model.

Culture and Personality: Developed by A.F.C. Wallace, holds that culture serves as a mediator between several personalities. Rejects the necessity of a **modal personality.**

Evolutionary Psychology: Psychological anthropologists of this school of thought postulate that independent **modules** in the brain, including the linguistic module, adapted humans to dominant environmental conditions during the Lower Paleolithic.

Folk Taxonomy (Psychological Anthropology): Studies investigating the idea that similar taxonomies of natural phenomena are likely to be found in different cultures.

Freudian Structure of Personality: An attempt to cast behavior in terms of developmental biology, postulates a three-fold personality structure comprising the *id*, or pure psychic energy; the *ego*, which mediates the relationship between desire and reality; and the *superego*, the moral component of the personality.

Genetic Causation: The theory that holds that genetic composition determines personality or intelligence, as articulated in such works as *The Bell Curve* by Charles Murray and Richard Herrnstein (1994).

Jen: The psychological interface in the human personality between internal psychobiological processes and external social ones, which form the personage of each individual, as suggested by Hsu.

Modal Personality: The statistically dominant personality type in a given culture. Expressed in statistical terms, the central tendency of a defined frequency distribution of one personality type or another within a culture.

National Character: Basic personality traits attributed to citizens of a nation.

Twin Studies: First initiated at the University of Minnesota. Holds that identical or **monozygotic** twins, but not fraternal (**dizygotic**) twins, who are reared separately, are likely to display similar personality traits.

Mental and Personality Disorders

Amok: A disorder, predominately among males, that begins with withdrawn behavior followed by a burst of violent, homicidal behavior in which the subject grabs a knife and stabs persons and objects within reach. Depression and amnesia follow the outburst.

Anorexia Nervosa: Disorder among young North American females whose preoccupation with thinness compels them to refuse to eat. Often followed by death, such as occurred with the singer, Karen Carpenter.

Arctic Hysteria (known as **pibloktoq** among Inuit and other names among other circumpolar peoples): A disorder brought on by fright followed by a variety of bizarre behaviors, such as tearing off clothes, jumping into water or fire, or thrashing about and speaking in tongues. Subject returns to normal behavior after the outburst. Among Reindeer Tungus, this behavior is a sign that the subject has been selected to become a shaman by virtue of contact with the unseen spirit world.

Diagnostic Statistical Manual of Mental Disorders Vol. 4 (DSM-IV): Standard manual adopted by the American Psychiatric Association that defines mental disorders recognized by consensus among professional members of the association.

Ethnic Psychoses: Mental disorders attributed to specific ethnic groups.

Windigo: Fear among Algonkian Indians of the northeastern United States and eastern Canada that monsters with a craving for human flesh will turn an individual into a cannibal. There is little evidence that cannibalism was practiced among Algonkian peoples.

Chapter 15
Anthropology of the Supernatural

General Terms

Contagious Magic: Ritual on body parts (nails, hair) or possessions of the target. More generally, the belief that things once in contact with each other can influence each other after separation.

Magic: The manipulation of supernatural beings and objects.

Noumena: Things and events in a world incapable of sensory perception, as opposed to phenomena, or things and events that can be perceived by the senses.

Religion: The supernatural world view that involves recognition of the unseen world and its beings, but does not involve direct manipulation. The emphasis lies on coming to terms with the unseen through supplication to the beings in the form of prayer and ritual. It should be noted that this is not an entirely clear distinction, and some anthropologists would reject this distinction altogether.

Sympathetic Magic: Magic that involves the belief that like produces like: the stereotypical practice of inserting pins into a likeness of the victim is one example. Also known as *imitative magic*.

Supernatural Forces and Beings

Demons: Beings that bring about evil, decay, or destruction; some have a supreme being of evil, such as Satan in Christianity, Judaism, and Islam.

Ghosts: Supernatural beings of human origin; many definitions emphasize malevolent qualities, perhaps present because of some unresolved wrong committed against them.

Gods: Supernatural beings, generically, of nonhuman origin.

Mana: Forces which are inanimate, that is, have no personality. Derived from the Polynesian, which entails the tabu of objects that have too much force (mana) for commoners to handle. May be compared with electricity, which is invisible but dangerous to those untrained to handle it.

Monotheism: Belief in one god only.

Polytheism: Belief in multiple gods, often specializing in different realms of human existence.

Spirits: Supernatural beings, usually of human and local origin; refers to ancestral spirits who may visit their localities of origin, such as Balinese or of Latin countries during Day of the Dead (November 1).

Supernatural Beings: Those perceived as supernatural persons, or at least attributed with a personality or personage.

Magical Practitioners and Practices

Black Magic: Manipulation of supernatural forces intended to bring harm to others; often equated to **sorcery** and **sorcerers.**

Divination: A belief that the cause of a particular event, such as illness, can be diagnosed by supernatural means or that the future can be foretold.

Shaman: Supernatural specialist practitioner who acts as mediator between spirit and material world; often involved with diagnosis, healing, or both.

Sorcery: Supernatural practice manipulating the supernatural with the intent to bring harm to others by ritual means; practitioners are called *sorcerers.*

White Magic: Manipulation of supernatural forces intended to benefit others.

Witchcraft: Supernatural forces unleashed, according to some definitions, that bring harm to others through attitudes or ill feeling on the part of the perpetrator, or *witch,* rather than performance of actual rituals. (Classic definition: poison oracle among Azande—chicken and strychnine, as reported by Evans-Pritchard). Other definitions equate witchcraft to *sorcery.*

Religion and World View

Animatism: Belief in impersonal supernatural forces in the surroundings (R. Marratt).

Animism: Belief in live beings in all phenomena; derived from dreams (E.B. Tylor).

Cosmic Religion: Body of beliefs, concepts, and rituals that are integrated into the natural environment, seasonal cycles, and all living lifeforms.

Dreamtime: Animistic system of belief among Australian Aborigines.

Ecclesiastical Religions: Religions that draw no distinctions between state and church, mosque, or other institution of worship.

Ethnoscience: Construction of the "world out there" in native thought.

Revitalization Movements: Movements involving the supernatural that arise when cultures are undergoing a rapid change. Examples: the cargo cults of New Guinea, the ghost dance of the Lakota Indians in the nineteenth century, and even the movement of the Branch Davidians in the early 1990s.

Theocracies: Governmental bodies consisting of priests or other leaders who derive their power from religion.

Universalistic Religions: Religions purporting to represent all humankind: Christianity, Judaism, Islam, and other so-called world religions are examples.

Case Studies

Dharma: The belief in the necessity of performing one's appointed duties in the current life.

Five Pillars of Islam: The obligations to invoke the name of God (Allah) every day, pray five times daily toward Mecca, provide alms for the poor, observe the fast during the lunar month of Ramadan, and to make at least one pilgrimage (*hajj*) to Mecca in a lifetime if one can afford it.

Jihad: Although popular conception regards it a call to struggle against the "infidels," its more basic meaning is the struggle against oneself in one's belief.

Karma: In Hinduism and Buddhism, the belief that all present lives are the consequences of good deeds and ill of past lives.

Nirvana: The realization that this world is illusion and the discovery of the reality beyond this illusory world.

Samsara: The belief that this world is a cosmic illusion.

Syncretism: The combination of two or more supernatural beliefs, such as folk Catholicism in Latin America and the combination of Islamic belief with *jinn* spirits in much of the Middle East.

Chapter 16
Globalization, Sociocultural Change, and Applied Anthropology

General Terms

Acculturation: Generic meaning: Changes induced in one or more than one culture through contact. According to some, forced change through intensive, firsthand contact between societies (Haviland 2002:487).

Modernization: The process of cultural and socioeconomic change whereby developing cultures adopt attributes of Western culture (from Haviland 2002:440).

Globalization and Its Discontents

Corporations: Under commercial law, an entity defined as a legal person, with limited liability, together with certain rights and obligations pertaining to its operations.

Global Level of Integration: The integration of the economic, political, and military forces on a worldwide scale.

Global Production System: An arrangement whereby industries have established *maquiladoras* throughout the world in an effort to capture cheap labor, with parts of the labor process distributed across nations according to cost considerations. Also known as the *international division of labor.* This system has been facilitated by recent innovations in transportation and telecommunications (as you know from using the Internet).

Imperialism: Policies of dominant nation states to gain indirect control of the economy of another nation state or by direct territorial acquisition.

Maquiladoras: Following the name given to factories in Mexico established near the U.S. border, any plant that performs part of the productive process for *transnational corporations* within the context of a *global production system.* They do not necessarily have to be located near the borders of developed countries.

Mercantilism: Policies of dominant nation states that include direct administrative and monopolistic control over the economy of another state, usually its colony.

Multinational Corporations: Corporations with operations in two or more nation states.

Trade-Related Intellectual Property Rights Agreement (TRIPS): part of the Marrakech Agreement signed off by member nations of the World Trade Organization, is designed to prevent underdeveloped countries from copying or stealing proprietary technology, but also claims proprietary rights over the less developed countries' (LDCs') natural resources.

Transnational Corporations: Corporations with highly integrated operations extending throughout two or more nation states.

Environmental Impact of Globalization

Global Warming: Also known as the **Greenhouse Effect,** the rise in the average temperature such that glaciers and the polar ice caps are melting, extreme weather is reported around the globe, and Pacific islands are under threat of seawater flooding.

Ozone Depletion: The thinning of the ozone layer, which filters three kinds of ultraviolet radiation, as the result of increased chlorofluorocarbons in the atmosphere.

Peak Oil: The point in the cycle of oil production and use where oil ceases to be cheap and plentiful and begins to be irreversibly more expensive and scarce. China's and India's recently increased demand for oil is exacerbating the shortage.

Population Growth: The exponential growth in world population from 1 billion in 1850, to 6 billion as of the year 2000 with projected growth to be 10.5 billion by 2050.

Population Replacement: An equilibrium between birth and death rates such that populations neither increase nor decrease. China's one-child policy is an attempt to achieve this goal.

Globalization: Local and Regional Effects

Cargo: Any of several religious and civil offices in which the holder, unpaid for his services, was obliged to pay for the offices' functions, often incurring a substantial debt at the end of the year; the cargo system was widespread throughout Mesoamerica and the Andes.

Closed Corporate Peasant Communities: Often an adaptation to colonization, communities which controlled the resources of its constituent members and their interaction with outsiders; in Mesoamerica, this was done with the *cargo* system. A similar corporate structure has been described for Central Java (Wolf 1957).

Enclosures: In England from the 15th Century onward, the displacement of common lands open to all peasants by private property (hence the term) which were fenced off for use of the gently and former lords, primarily for raising sheep and other livestock.

Extermination: The mass murder of peoples within a given territory, such as the frequent massacres of Native people in North America and Australia.

Genocide: The deliberate mass murder of one ethnic group by another, often in the name of socioeconomic development or "progress," with the express aim of eliminating that population.

Peasantization (also known as de-agrarianization): The process of cultural change whereby former independent horticulturalists are forcibly linked to the state through taxation, marketization, or other means.

Proletarianization: The process of cultural change whereby former independent horticulturalists or peasants lose their land or other resources and become dependent on the labor market.

Rural-to-Urban Migration: A worldwide trend for former agrarian peoples to migrate to the cities as they lose their lands and other resources in rural areas as part of the **proletarianization** process.

Slavery: The forced and involuntary servitude of a population, such as blacks in West Africa during the period from the sixteenth to the nineteenth century; there are signs of a resurgence of slavery in the present.

State Terrorism: The deliberate use of lethal force by a national government to control or eliminate selected populations within states, such as the *kulaks* (wealthy peasants) in the Soviet Union under Stalin, the Armenian genocide in 1915 Turkey, or the extermination of the Jews under Nazi Germany.

Structural Violence: Violence generated by economic, political, and social structures and institutions. Classic examples: low wages in the **maquiladoras** in underdeveloped countries that fail to provide the basic necessities for the workers; murders of those involved in movements for social justice, such as the 500,000 known assassinations and "disappearances" during the hidden civil war in Guatemala (1960–1996).

Villagization: The process of cultural change whereby formerly nomadic peoples are persuaded or forced to move into villages. Found largely in countries of East Africa, the Middle East, and former Soviet republics, such as Uzbekistan and Kazakhstan.

Theories of Socioeconomic Change and Development

Core Countries: Countries with diversified economies and advanced industry that include the United States, Canada, Great Britain, France, Germany, northern Italy, and Japan. Some would also include Russia (especially during its Soviet phase).

Demonstration Effect: A concomitant of **diffusion,** the desire by the client or target group to accept an innovation whose advantages are obvious, or at least apparent.

Dependency Theory: The theory that the development of industrialized societies came at the deprivation of underdeveloped countries, which rely on a single resource (coffee, bananas, tin, copper, oil). Articulated by Andre Gunder Frank.

Diffusion: From anthropology, the spread of practices, customs, or technology from one culture to another. If the new element is an innovative technique or object with evident benefit, the term **demonstration effect** often applies. George Foster lists among the barriers to change the **image of limited good** and the **dyadic contract.**

Dyadic Contract: The practice, attributed to peasant or other "traditional" societies, that agreements involve two, and only two, persons, making it easier to escape the agreement if it proves disadvantageous to one of the parties.

Image of Limited Good: Beliefs attributed to peasant or other "traditional" societies that desirable qualities exist only in fixed amounts incapable of increase. Represents a variation of the zero-sum game which one person's gain is another person's loss.

Localocentrism: An excessive focus among social researchers on local communities with little attention devoted to socioeconomic forces that originate outside a given community but encroach upon that community.

Need for Achievement (n-ach): Postulated by McClelland, the notion that "traditional" societies whose members show a drive for accomplishment are the best candidates for development aid. McClelland posits a number of indicators for this "need for achievement" (*n*-achievement or *n*-ach), such as folk tales.

Pattern Variables: From sociology, the notion that indices can measure extremes between "traditional" and "modern" society. Examples: ascription (being born into a task, such as an occupational caste in India) versus achievement (acquiring a position by training and demonstrated accomplishments); particularlism (gaining a position by personal contact: "who you know") versus universalism (gaining a position by meeting requirements by criteria applicable to all: "what you know").

Peripheral Countries: Countries that rely on a single resource for export; at one time, the country was identified with its leading export: Guatemala (coffee), Chile (copper), Argentina (beef and grains), Bolivia (tin), and Zambia (copper) are among the classic examples.

Primary Innovation: The discovery of a new principle or technology.

Secondary Innovation: The application of a new principle or technology to a society or culture, inducing change in that society or culture.

Semi-Peripheral Countries: Countries occupying an intermediate position between **core countries** and **peripheral countries,** both in terms of levels of development (some industry is present) and in roles as conduits between the other two types of countries.

Stage Theory of Economic Growth: Postulated by Rostow, a fivefold stage theory of economic development from the traditional to the age of high mass consumption.

World Systems Analysis: The theory, elaborated from **dependency theory,** which divides the global economy into **core countries** that draw resources and exploit the cheap labor in **peripheral countries** through the conduits that involve **semi-peripheral countries.** Articulated by Immanuel Wallerstein and his associates.

Applied Anthropology

Applied Anthropology: The application of anthropological knowledge to problems and their solutions, usually in non-Western cultures. Much of applied anthropology involves persuasion of those societies to accept the Western model, including orientation of society to Western-dominant market systems.

Forensics: Science of crime scene reconstruction using skeletal and dental analysis, together with the cause of death; physical anthropology plays a significant role in this discipline.

Medical Anthropology: A discipline combining physical and cultural anthropology that applies findings about folk medical beliefs to actual treatment, including such areas as biomedicine, ethnomedicine, and alternative systems of medical care.

Vicos Project (Cornell-Peru Project): A classical case study in **applied anthropology** of an hacienda that was transformed from a feudal estate to a commercial farm owned and operated by the former peasants. Despite its evident success, the Peruvian government blocked efforts in other peasant communities to emulate the CPP.

ALPHABETICAL GLOSSARY IN ANTHROPOLOGY

A

Abbevillian Tradition: A period that included manufacture of asymmetrical handaxes, possibly a transition between the **Oldowan** and **Acheulean traditions.**

Acculturation: Generic meaning: Changes induced in one or more than one culture through contact. According to some, forced change through intensive, firsthand contact between societies (Haviland 2002:487).

Acheulean Tradition: A major archaeological culture of the Lower Paleolithic, whose definitive artifact is a well-crafted, symmetrical handaxe. None was found to the east of the **Movius Line.**

Achievement: Assignment to a category based on the person's own efforts, such as an occupational association or union, political party, or interest group such as the Benevolent League of Terminators.

Adjudication: Mediation in which the neutral party makes the final decision. Usually associated with a chiefdom or state society.

Affines (Affinal Kin): Those kin linked by marriage ties: wife-husband, in-laws.

Affix: A **bound morpheme** that modifies the meaning or syntactic subcategory of the **base** in some way.

Affluence Hypothesis: Hypothesis that **foraging** peoples have few needs for which a low-yield technology suffices.

Age Division of Labor: The assignment of tasks based on age. The most demanding tasks are assigned to young to middle-aged adults.

Age Grades: Among East African societies, of which Tiriki of Kenya stand as an example, fixed 15-year categories (boys; warriors; elder warriors; judicial elders; ritual elders; and 2 categories of retired and deceased men). Refers to fixed age categories in any society, but East African societies serve as classical examples.

Age Sets: Again as illustrated by the Tiriki of Kenya, movable categories of men who change age grades every fifteen years. Any society with movable age categories, of which East African societies serve as classical examples.

Allele: One of a pair of **genes** that codes for variations of a specific trait in the organism.

Allen's Rule: A theory predicting that within the same species, the relative size of protruding parts of the body, such as nose and ears, and the relative length of the arms and legs, increases as the average environmental temperature increases.

Allomorph: One of two or more variants of the smallest unit of meaning. Example: differences in suffixes of cats, dogs, and horses, which end, respectively, in -s, -z, and -ez (when pronounced).

Allophones: The speech sound variants of the same phoneme. Example: aspirated [kʰ] in key and teak; unaspirated [k⁻] in ski. Note the two k's never occur in the same speech environment.

All-Purpose or **Multipurpose Money:** Money used for making payment for all, or almost all, goods and services. U.S. currency is one example.

Alveolar Ridge: The gum ridge behind the upper teeth.

Ambilineal, Cognatic, or **Nonunilinear Descent Groups:** Descent groups of bilateral kin who, by selection, demonstrate or stipulate their descent from a common ancestor through a combination of male and female kin.

Ambilineal Descent: A form of bilateral descent in which an individual may opt to affiliate with either the father's or the mother's descent group.

Ambilocal Residence: One in which the couple lives with the kin of one or the other; the choice is made situationally (one or the other household has more land, etc.).

Amitilocal Residence: One in which the couple theoretically lives with the wife's father's sister; a theoretical construct, no known example exists.

Amok: A disorder, predominately among males, that begins with withdrawn behavior followed by a burst of violent, homicidal behavior in which the subject grabs a knife and stabs persons and objects within reach. Depression and amnesia follow the outburst.

Angular Gyrus: Area located in the parietal region, whose role it is to integrate multimodal (i.e., sight, sound, touch, taste, and smell) information from the senses.

Animalia: Lifeforms of a kingdom that feed on other lifeforms, are incapable of producing their own food, and are motile, or mobile.

Animatism: Belief in impersonal supernatural forces in the surroundings. (R. Marratt).

Animism: Belief in live beings in all phenomena; derived from dreams (E.B. Tylor).

Anorexia Nervosa: Disorder among young North American females whose preoccupation with thinness compels them to refuse to eat. Often followed by death, such as occurred with the singer, Karen Carpenter.

Anthropoidea: Monkeys, apes, and humans, but not prosimians, which belong to that **suborder.**

Anthropology: The **holistic** and comparative study of humankind.

Apex: Tip of the tongue.

Apico-Alveolar Stop: Formed by the closure of the tip or **apex** of the tongue with gum or **alveolar ridge.**

Applied Anthropology: The application of anthropological knowledge to problems and their solution, usually in non-Western cultures. Much of applied anthropology involves persuasion of those societies to accept the Western model, including orientation of society to Western-dominant market systems.

Arbitrariness: The absence of a relationship between an act of communication (speech utterance) and its meaning. Acts of communication with intrinsic meanings are called iconic.

Arch (Human Foot): The double curvature on the human foot: the longitudinal arch along the foot lengthwise, and the transverse arch across the center of the foot.

Archaeology: The comparative study primarily of cultural remains of human societies, although the study of fossil hominids (earlier human and humanlike forms) relevant to material culture (e.g., tool making) is also included.

Arctic Hysteria (known as **pibloktoq** among Inuit and other names among other circumpolar peoples): A disorder brought on by fright followed by a variety of bizarre behaviors, such as tearing off clothes, jumping into water or fire, or thrashing about and speaking in tongues. Subject returns to normal behavior after the outburst. Among Reindeer Tungus, this behavior is a sign that the subject has been selected to become a shaman by virtue of contact with the unseen spirit world.

Arcuate Fasciculus: Bundle of nerves that connects *Broca's area* and *Wernicke's area.*

Articulate: (verb) To speak; the movement of parts of the speech mechanism in speaking.

Articulators: Parts in the lower part of the mouth involved in articulation. These include the lower lip, lower teeth, tip or **apex** of tongue, **front** or **blade** of tongue, center or **centrum** of tongue, and back or **dorsum** of tongue. See diagram (Fig. 4.1) of text.

Ascription: Assignment to a social category at birth, such as gender or, as time goes on, by age.

Aspirated Utterance: Those involving strong expulsion of air.

Australopithecines: Generic category that includes both *Australopithecus* and *Paranthropus.*

Australopithecus. A genus comprising early hominids with bipedalism, lower *cranial capacity,* and no direct evidence of stone tool manufacture and use. Include *Australopithecus afarensis, Australopithecus africanus, Australopithecus garhi,* and others. *Lumpers* would include *Paranthropus* as well.

Authority: In asymmetrical political relations, the process of security compliance by persuasion. Examples range from headman leadership in tribal societies to political campaigns in modern society. Sometimes associated with *cultural control,* or control through a set of shared values and beliefs internalized by members of a culture.

Avunculocal Residence: One in which the couple lives with or near the husband's mother's brother. Occurs in matrilineal societies.

B

Balanced Reciprocity: Direct exchange of goods and services of more or less equal value, and where tabs are kept. Classic example: Melanesian Kula Ring.

Band: A small nomadic group (averaging around 50), comprising several households, that either lack headmen or includes headmen lacking power and whose influence is derived from persuasion.

Barter: The direct exchange of a good or service for another without money.

Base: The **morpheme** to which an **affix** is added (e.g., *cat* is the base to which the **affix -*s*** is added to form a plural. In this case, the affix is a **suffix.). Sometimes also known as the root.**

Behavior: Person's expression of an outward manifestation of the first three elements of personality (**perception, cognition,** and **emotion**).

Behavioral Environment: The world of objects other than self, mediated symbolically through language.

Berdaches: Among Plains Indians, men who took on women's dress and tasks.

Bifurcate Collateral Terminology: Aunt/uncle terminology which father, mother, father's brother, mother's sister, mother's brother, and father's sisters are all distinguished from each other.

Bifurcate Merging Terminology: Aunt/uncle terminology in which mother's brother and father's sisters are distinguished from father's brother and mother's sister, who are not distinguished from father or mother.

Bifurcation: Terminological distinction between relatives on the father's side from relatives on the mother's side.

Big Man: In New Guinea, a man with influence who mobilizes and manipulates wealth on behalf of his group to sponsor major feasts that enhance his prestige relative to other big men.

Bilabial Stop: Stop formed by closure between upper and lower lips; full term is **labio-labial stop.**

Bilateral Decent: The rule by which kin are reckoned through both male and female links equally; distance, that is, degrees of removal, rather than sex of connecting link, is used to differentiate kin.

Bilateral Cross-Cousin Marriage: Marriage of a man to a woman who is either his father's sister's daughter or mother's brother's daughter—and who may, in some societies, be both (as among the Yanomamö).

Bilateral Kindred: A group of kin related to a set of full brothers and sisters.

Bipedalism: The ability to walk on two feet. The structure of almost the entire skeleton is oriented around this ability.

Black Magic: Manipulation of supernatural forces intended to bring harm to others; often equated to **sorcery** and **sorcerers.**

Blade (Linguistics): Another term for **front** of tongue.

Blade (Tool): A characteristic tool in later periods of the **Paleolithic;** a **flake** whose length is at least twice its width.

Blended Family: Combined family or couple, each with her and/or his own children from previous marriages.

Body: Another term for **centrum** of tongue.

Bound Morpheme: A **morpheme** that must be attached to another morpheme (e.g., the plural marker *-s* as in *cats*).

Brahmin: Priestly **caste,** the topmost of the hierarchy of Indian castes.

Brainstem: Part of the brain that is involved with some of the body functions essential to life; breathing and the heartbeat are examples.

Breeding Population: Within a species, a community of individuals where mates are usually found.

Bride Labor: Practice whereby the groom works for the bride's family or wider kin before taking his bride to his own place of residence. Often associated with **matri-patrilocal residence** whereby a couple lives with the wife's family before living with the husband's family.

Bridewealth: (sometimes also known by the less accurate term **Brideprice):** Payment to the bride's family or larger kin group at the time of the marriage. Known by its Swahili term **lobola** reflecting its widespread practice in East Africa.

Broca's Area: Area in the **left hemisphere** that is involved with the production of spoken language.

Burakumin: A Japanese **caste** considered inferior to all other Japanese; like the Indian **Dalits,** they engage in "unclean" occupations such as leatherworking and are isolated in ghettos.

C

Calcaneus: Heel bone of the foot.

Canine Teeth: Jagged teeth immediately behind the *incisors,* which perform piercing functions.

Capital: Goods or services intended for production of further goods and services; claims over such goods and services, such as money, stocks, and bonds.

Capitalism: The private ownership of resources and equipment intended for production.

Capitalist Mode of Production: A system of production under **capitalism** in which goods and services are produced for the market, usually by workers lacking means of production other than their labor. The model is M-C-M', where M means money, C means commodity, and M' means increased amounts of money. The aim is to realize a profit.

Cargo: Any of several religious and civil offices in which the holder, unpaid for his services, was obliged to pay for the offices' functions, often incurring a substantial debt at the end of the year; the cargo system was widespread throughout Mesoamerica and the Andes.

Carrying Capacity: The number of people who can be supported by the available resources at a given level of technology.

Caste: A social class, within a system of stratification, to which membership is determined by birth and in which the individual remains for life. By definition, such groups are *endogamous.* Indian is best known for its caste system, but Japan also discriminates against *Burakumin* (Japan's "untouchables") and the physically different Ainu.

Catarrhini: Old World monkeys, apes, and humans, all with projecting noses and nostrils pointed downward, all which belong to that *infraorder.* This category excludes all New World Monkeys, which have flat noses and therefore categorized as Platyrrhini.

Cell: The smallest unit capable of performing all functions of a living organism.

Centrum: Central part of the tongue, sometimes known as the **body.**

Cerebellum: Part of the brain immediately above the brainstem which regulates all aspects of body movement, including balance and body position.

Cerebrum: Enlarged anterior of the brain that overlies the other parts of the brain, considered to be the seat of conscious mental processes.

Cervical Vertebrae: Neck bones of the *vertebrae.*

Chiefdom: A ranked society with a head whose office is permanent and involves a rule of succession.

Childhood Familiarity Explanation: The explanation that the **incest tabu** arises from the lack of interest or revulsion of sexual behavior between siblings or other individuals reared together from childhood (such as those on an Israeli kibbutz).

Chin: Bony protuberance projecting outward from the mandible that reinforces the two halves of that mandible; a sure indication that the specimen is modern *Homo sapiens*.

Chinampas: Raised fields constructed from alternate layers of earth and decayed vegetation to form a rich—and relatively dry—platform for the crops.

Chordata: Animals with spinal cords. Humans belong to that *phylum.*

Chrometrics: Study of the social perception of time.

Chromosomes: Strings of hereditary material, made up of **DNA,** which contain the codes for all physical traits of the organism.

Circumscription: The hemming in of a society by geographical barriers, such as mountains, large bodies of water, or desert, such that few options are open to the subjects of a **state** thereby allowing its formation and persistence.

Cladistics: Classification system based on order of evolutionary branching based on genetics instead of present similarities and differences.

Clans: *Unilineal* descent groups whose members reckon descent through assumed, though unknown links *(stipulated)* in the male or female line to a common ancestor. In American usage, also known as *Sibs.*

Class (Taxonomic): A subcategory of *subphylum* (or superclass, as the case may be) which includes *Mammalia.*

Classificatory Terms: Kinship terms that refer to a wide range of relatives. Example is *cousin* in English, which covers mother's brother's, father's, sister's and others' offspring of both sexes.

Closed-Class Society: A society in which **social mobility** is rare or nonexistent.

Closed Corporate Peasant Communities: Often an adaptation to colonization, communities which controlled the resources of its constituent members and their interaction with outsiders; in Mesoamerica, this was done with the *cargo* system. A similar corporate structure has been described for Central Java (Wolf 1957).

Closed Systems (Linguistics): Communication systems whose elements cannot be combined with others to form a third meaning.

Coccyx: Tailbone; the tip of the lower vertebrae.

Code Switching: The practice of changing from one type of language system or dialect to another. For example, Martin Luther King spoke Afro-American English to a black audience and standard formal English to a white or mixed audience.

Codified Law: Written or at least carefully stated law that defines civil breaches and crimes and that specifies the remedies—lawsuit settlements or punishments—for each.

Codominant (Genetics): (adj.) The situation in which, in a **heterozygous** individual, both alleles are expressed in the phenotype.

Cognition: Thought processes involved in interpreting one's **perception** of the world.

Cognitive Development: The phases of acquiring cognitive abilities in the Piagetan **sensorimotor phase, preoperational phase, concrete-operational phase,** and the **formal-operational phase.**

Collateral Kin: Kin descended from a common ancestor with Ego, but who are not ego's direct ascendants or descendants. Examples are Ego's siblings.

Color Cognition: Studies claiming that cultures categorize colors in similar ways depending on industrial development; from two basic colors among foragers to eleven among industrialized peoples.

Command Economy: Economy in which goods and services are controlled by a state; examples are modern socialist states and possibly the Inca, both of which relied primarily on **redistribution.**

Commodities: Goods and services produced primarily for sale on the market.

Common-Interest Associations: Associations based on interests other than age, gender, kinship, or territory; resulting from the act of joining.

Communalism: Ownership of property by a culture at large, such as the hunting territories of the Southwestern African !Kung and other foraging societies. One variation of this involves communal tenure in which individuals have use rights, or rights of **usufruct.**

Communication: An act by which one organism triggers another.

Compatibility With Child Care Explanation: An explanation for the **gender** division of labor in that women tend to handle tasks that they can interrupt to attend to their children.

Complementary Opposition: A characteristic of **segmentary lineages** in which kinship groups of equal scope may become allies or opponents, depending on the issue at hand.

Complex Foraging: Subtype of **foraging** based on high-yield and/or reliable food sources that enable populations to stay at one location; Northwest Coast Native peoples, who relied on regular salmon runs, are examples.

Comprehensiveness: The rule whereby a proposition must be tested by all relevant information and data, by those that not only support the proposition but also those that do not support it.

Concrete-Operational Phase: Age (7–11 years) at which children begin to connect events in terms of cause and effect, and they begin to manipulate symbols in a more nuanced way.

Concubines: Women cohabiting with men without being legally married; a common practice among royal or aristocratic males in China, for example.

Conical Clan: Clan whose constituent lineages are ranked by closeness to the chief lineage, one maintained by lines of eldest sons to the presumed ancestor.

Consanguine Family: A family comprising related women, their brothers, and the women's offspring. Usually found in association with matrilineal descent.

Consanguines (Consanguineal Kin): Those kin linked by "blood" ties: parent-child (generational) or those of brothers and/or sisters (sibling[s]), or both.

Consensus: The decision-making process based on the consent of all present before embarking on a course of action.

Consonants: Sounds that are produced with a narrow, partial, or complete closure in the **vocal tract.**

Contagious Magic: Ritual on body parts (nails, hair) or possessions of the target. More generally, the belief that things once in contact with each other can influence each other after separation.

Core: Stone from which **flakes** or chips are **flintknapped** with a **hammerstone.** A core may or may not be fashioned into a tool.

Core Countries: Countries with diversified economies and advanced industry that include the United States, Canada, Great Britain, France, Germany, northern Italy, and Japan. Some would also include Russia (especially during its Soviet phase).

Core Values: Those values held highest within a given culture.

Core Vocabulary: Part of glottochronology, the pronouns, lower numerals, and nouns of body parts and natural objects used to reconstruct linguistic commonalities and divergence.

Corporate Group: An organized group of kin who controls an estate, exists in perpetuity as a corporate "person," and maintains a body of rights and obligations that extends to all its members as a unit.

Corporations: Under commercial law, an entity defined as a legal person, with limited liability, together with certain rights and obligations pertaining to its operations.

Corpus Callosium: Nerve fibers connecting the two **hemispheres** of the brain.

Cosmic Religion: Body of beliefs, concepts, and rituals that are integrated into the natural environment, seasonal cycles, and all living lifeforms.

Craft Specialization: Assignment of tasks according to ability and training.

Cranium (pl. Crania): The skull or, more specifically, the part of the skull housing the brain; the braincase.

Critical Period of Language Acquisition: Period of time between birth and puberty in which language acquisition must take place, according to the linguist Noam Chomsky.

Cross-Cousins: Ego's father's sister or mother's brother's child.

Cross-Cultural Comparison: The comparison of two or more cultures with regard to a certain trait or complex of traits. If any generalization is to hold up for all the peoples of the world, then it must be tested with instances from several cultures.

Crow System: A mode of kinship reckoning, associated with matrilineal descent, in which a father's sister and father's sister's daughter are called by the same term, a mother and mother's sister are merged under another term, and a father and father's brother are merged into a third. Parallel cousins are equated with brothers and sisters.

Crystalline Stone: Stone containing grain that enables the stone to fracture in a predictable way. Examples are flint, obsidian, chert, agate, and slate.

Cultural Anthropology (also known as **sociocultural anthropology** and **ethnology**): The comparative study of human behavior according to the rules, usually implicit, of the society of which individuals are a part.

Cultural Configuration: A hypothesis first advanced by Ruth Benedict that a culture is a "personality writ large," whereby a culture represents the sum total of the personalities of the people who compose it; precursor of *modal personality* model.

Cultural Materialism: A theoretical orientation that focuses on technoenvironmental factors as key determinants in cultural adaptation and evolution.

Cultural Relativism: Cultural relativism refers to the idea that, because all cultures are unique, they can be evaluated only according to their own standards and values. Interpretations range from the **Noble Savage Complex** that sees "primitive" societies as free from the corrupting influences of civilization to an anthropological version of **scientific detachment,** or the open-mindness that is characteristic of scientific inquiry.

Cultural Transmission: Acquisition of an element of communication by learning, and with a propensity to change.

Cultural Universalism: The idea that all people, regardless of culture, have many things in common. An imperfect opposite to *cultural relativism* but without the notion of the superiority of one's culture.

Culture (E.B. Tylor, founder of anthropology in Great Britain): "That complex whole which includes knowledge, belief, art, law, morals, custom, and any other capabilities and habits acquired by man as a member of society."

Culture (Haviland): The values, beliefs, and perceptions of the world shared by members of a society that they use to interpret experience and generate behavior and that are reflected in their behavior (2002:34). Cultures are learned, symbolic, shared, patterned, and generally adaptive. See text for explanation.

Culture and Personality: Developed by A.F.C. Wallace, holds that culture serves as a mediator between several personalities. Rejects the necessity of a *modal personality*.

Culture Bound: (adj.) Related to ethnocentrism, but with the interpretation that all phenomena are "screened" through one's own "cultural filters," whether such screening is conscious or not.

Cytoplasm: All the material found in a gelatin-like substance between the membrane of the nucleus and the wall of the cell.

D

Dalit: A member of an "untouchable" **caste** in India who is thought to pollute members of other (**varna**) castes by his or her presence, and pursues occupations considered "polluting," such as leatherworking. The term *Harijan* also applied to this caste.

Deep Structure: The structure that all languages share, from which rules of transformation serve to generate the **surface structure** of a specific language.

Deleterious Mutation: A *mutation* that renders an organism maladaptive to a given environment. Most mutations are deleterious.

Demand: The willingness and ability to purchase a good or service at a given price.

Demons: Beings that bring about evil, decay, or destruction; some have a supreme being of evil, such as Satan in Christianity, Judaism, and Islam.

Demonstrated Descent: Tracing of descent through known links to a given ancestor.

Demonstration Effect: A concomitant of **diffusion,** the desire by the client or target group to accept an innovation whose advantages are obvious, or at least apparent.

Dental Arcade: The arrangement of teeth on a jaw; the dental arcade of prehuman primates tends to be rectangular, with the back teeth running parallel; that of middle and recent hominids tends to be rounded.

Dental Formula: The number of *incisors, canines, premolars,* and *molars* on one side of the upper and lower jaw. Humans, apes, and Old World monkey's formula is the same: 2.1.2.3 on each side of each jaw; New World monkeys' formula varies from this formula.

Deoxyribonucleic Acid (DNA): Long double spirals of molecules comprising sugar and phosphate molecules, together with paired bases that link the two strands. Also known as **chromosomes,** DNA contains the codes for all physical traits of the organism.

Dependence Training: Child-rearing practices that foster compliance with the performance of assigned tasks and dependence on the domestic group, rather than reliance on oneself.

Dependency Theory: The theory that the development of industrialized societies came at the deprivation of underdeveloped countries, which rely on a single resource (coffee, bananas, tin, copper, oil). Articulated by Andre Gunder Frank.

Descent Group: A group of kin descended **unilineally** or **ambilineally** from a common ancestor.

Descriptive Linguistics: The description and analysis of the structure and content of an individual language.

Descriptive Terms: Kinship terms that refer to one or at most two kinds of relatives. Examples are *Father* and *Mother* in English terminology.

Detail Labor: Labor process in which tasks of a given craft are broken down to their constituent parts, with each part assigned to a worker or team of workers. A defining characteristic of industrial society.

Dharma: The belief in the necessity of performing one's appointed duties in the current life.

Diagnostic Statistical Manual of Mental Disorders Vol. 4 (DSM-IV): Standard manual adopted by the American Psychiatric Association that defines mental disorders recognized by consensus among professional members of the association.

Dialects: Varying forms of a language that reflect particular or social classes but that are similar enough to be mutually intelligible—Bargains on the West Coast become Bahgains in Bahston, MA. All dialects have the potential to become separate language in time.

Diaspora: The scattering of peoples of one ethnicity throughout a wide geographical area, even across the globe. Jews are a classic example, but blacks, Armenians, and overseas Chinese are other examples.

Diastema: In non-human primates and early hominids, the gap between the incisors and canine that accommodates the canine of the opposite jaw.

Diffusion: From anthropology, the spread of practices, customs, or technology from one culture to another. If the new element is an innovative technique or object with evident benefit, the term **demonstration effect** often applies. George Foster lists among the barriers to change the **image of limited good** and the **dyadic contract.**

Diploid: (adj.) Refers to double the number of chromosomes in an organism during **mitosis.**

Displacement: Ability to refer to things and events not immediately present.

Distribution of Wealth: The equal or differential control or ownership of assets, such as land, productive capital, money and other claims to wealth, and others. *See also* **Stratified Society** *and* **Social Class.**

Divination: A belief that the cause of a particular event, such as illness, can be diagnosed by supernatural means or that the future can be foretold.

Division of Labor: Assignment of tasks to individuals of certain categories based on some criteria.

Divorce: Dissolution of marriage, however defined, according to the norms of the society in which it occurs.

DNA: see *Deoxyribonucleic Acid.*

Domestic Mode of Production: Production oriented primarily for the household; production ceases when the needs of the household are met. The model of exchange is C-M-C, where the householder produces a good or service for sale to obtain another good or service the householder cannot produce.

Dominant (genetics): (adj) The situation in which, in a **heterozygous** individual, only one **allele** is expressed in the **phenotype.**

Dorso-Velar Stop: **Stop** formed by closure of back or **dorsum** of tongue with **velum** or soft palate.

Dorsum: Back part of the tongue.

Double Descent (Shorthand for *Double Unilineal Descent):* A system that affiliates an individual with a group of matrilineal kin for some purposes and with a group of patrilineal kin for other purposes.

Dowry: Transfer of wealth from bride's family or kin to groom or his kin upon marriage. Practiced in societies with intensive cultivation, as in European countries. The practice of the bride's father paying for the wedding is a holdover from this practice.

Dreamtime: Animistic system of belief among Australian Aborigines.

Duolocal Residence: One in which each of the couple lives with her (his) respective unilineal group; one spouse is regarded as a "guest" in the other's home during visits (this form of postmarital residence is rare).

Dyadic Contract: The practice, attributed to peasant or other "traditional" societies, that agreements involve two, and only two, persons, making it easier to escape the agreement if it proves disadvantageous to one of the parties.

E

Ecclesiastical Religions: Religions that draw no distinctions between state and church, mosque, or other institution of worship.

Economic Anthropology (Formal): The cross-cultural study of human behavior that involves the relationship between ends and scarce means that have alternative uses (from L. M. Robbins definition of "economic science").

Economic Anthropology (Substantive): The study of the production, distribution, and consumption of goods and services. Often confused with **technology,** as reflected in such terms as "a hunting-gathering economy" or "an agricultural economy."

Economic Goods: In economics, goods (and services) that exist in finite supply.

Economize: (verb) To maximize the use of one's assets.

Economy: The study of the provision, distribution, and consumption of goods and services.

Edge Hypothesis: Hypothesis on the invention of agriculture that suggests that land use became intensified at the edge of natural hunting and gathering habitats by populations that otherwise might have been forced out of such habitats.

Egalitarian Societies: Societies in which there are as many valued status positions as there are persons capable of filling them (Fried 1967); the **big man** complex in New Guinea is one example.

Egocentric Groups: Groups centered around an individual or group of individuals.

Emotions: One's affective response to, or feelings about, **perception** or **cognition** of a given situation.

Encephalization: The proportion of brain size relative to other measures, such as body size; also, the tendency of the human biological brain to increase in size.

Enclosures: In England from the 15th Century onward, the displacement of common lands open to all peasants by private property (hence the term) which were fenced off for use of the gently and former lords, primarily for raising sheep and other livestock.

Endogamy: Marriage within a particular group or category of individuals: within a village, band, **caste,** or other group.

Environment (Linguistics): The environment in which a **phone** occurs.

Epiglottis: Thin plate of flexible cartilage that folds back over and protects the glottis (space between vocal cords) during swallowing. Epiglottis and larynx are located in lower position in the respiratory system in humans than in other vertebrates, thereby increasing risk of choking.

Epiphytic Plants: In tropical regions, plants that anchor themselves in treetops but derive their primary moisture and nutrients from the atmosphere.

Equestrian Hunting: As the term implies, hunting using a domesticated horse or other draft animal. Plains Indians are an example.

Eskimo System: A mode of kinship reckoning in which mother, father, brother and sister are specifically identified. Mother is distinguished from aunts, father from uncles, and siblings from cousins. All other relatives are terminologically merged (for example parallel cousins are not distinguished from cross-cousins and uncles and aunts on one side of the family are not distinguished from the other side.)

Ethical Relativism: Defined as tolerance of practices harmful to the body or psyche of the victims.

Ethnic Discrimination: Discrimination exercised against specific ethnic groups. Example: In the Mexican state of Chiapas and in Guatemala, Ladinos (who may be biological Indians themselves) discriminate against Indians for their cultural practices rather than their physical characteristics.

Ethnic Preservation Societies: Often associated with cultural change, societies seeking to preserve indigenous traditions, such as the Tribal Unions of West Africa, the Mayan associations in Guatemala, and the several Native American associations.

Ethnic Psychoses: Mental disorders attributed to specific ethnic groups.

Ethnocentrism: The belief in the superiority of one's own culture over all other cultures.

Ethnolinguistics: The study of relations between language and culture.

Ethnoscience: Construction of the "world out there" in native thought.

Eugenics: A *pseudoscience* that attributes differences in behavior or personality characteristics, such as intelligence, to differences in physical characteristics and attempts to breed "pure" **races** on the basis of that belief.

Evolutionary Psychology: Psychological anthropologists of this school of thought postulate that independent *modules* in the brain, including the linguistic module, adapted humans to dominant environmental conditions during the Lower Paleolithic.

Exchange: The act of giving or taking a good or service in return for another. Sometimes used interchangeably with *Transaction,* whose connotation is within the context of modern business.

Exogamy: Marriage outside a particular group or category of individuals: family (almost always), lineage or clan (usually), village, or other group. Not to be confused with *incest,* which emphasizes sexual intercourse rather than marriage.

Extended Family: One made up of three or more generations of consanguineal kin (parents and children), together with their spouses.

Extermination: The mass murder of peoples within a given territory, such as the frequent massacres of Native people in North America and Australia.

F

Falsifiability: The rule whereby a proposition must be so stated that it is rejected if it fails to pass a test (in the laboratory or in the field).

Family: A subcategory of **superfamily** (taxonomies vary) that comprises all **hominids** (modern and fossil human forms), **Pongidae** (great apes) and **Hylobatidae** (gibbons, or lesser apes).

Femur: Thighbone.

Feud: A state of recurring hostilities between families, lineages, or other kin groups, usually the product of revenge and counter-revenge killings; among the Dani of Western New Guinea (Irian Jaya), revenge is obligatory, enforced by one's ancestral spirits.

Feudalism or Patrimonialism: An arrangement whereby a serf provides goods and services to the owner of a landed estate in return for protection and the right to use a portion of the owner's property.

Fibula: Smaller of the two leg bones, located at the rear.

Five Pillars of Islam: The obligations to invoke the name of God (Allah) every day, pray five times daily toward Mecca, provide alms for the poor, observe the fast during the lunar month of Ramadan, and to make at least one pilgrimage (*hajj*) to Mecca in a lifetime if one can afford it.

Flake: Stone chip **flintknapped** from a **core;** flakes may be further fashioned into a tool, or may be tossed aside as a **waste flake** or **debitage.**

Flintknapping: The process of making chipped stone artifacts; the striking of stone with a hard or soft hammer.

Flood Plain Irrigation: Irrigation in which fields are abandoned to flooding during the rainy season and planted when the flood recedes.

Folk Taxonomy (Psychological Anthropology): Studies investigating the idea that similar taxonomies of natural phenomena are likely to be found in different cultures.

Folk Taxonomy (Racial Categories): The classification of phenomena on the basis of cultural tradition; the concept of **Race** is one example.

Food Collection: Subsistence technology which involves primary reliance on naturally occurring food sources.

Food Production: Subsistence technology which involves primary reliance on domesticated plants, animals, or both.

Foraging or Hunting and Gathering: Dependence primarily or exclusively on hunting, fishing, and gathering. Also known as **food collection** in which food sources are those yielded by nature without human modification of the environment.

Foramen Magnum: Large hole at base of the human brain through which the **spinal cord** passes.

Forensics: Science of crime scene reconstruction using skeletal and dental analysis, together with the cause of death; physical anthropology plays a significant role in this discipline.

Form Classes: The parts of speech or categories of words that work the same way in any sentence (e.g., Noun Forms: "I see a _____ [dog, cat, mouse; each is substitutable for the other]"; Verb Forms: "I _____ a cat [see, chase, tackle; again, they are mutually substitutable; this process of substitution is called Frame Substitution]").

Formalism: The perspective in economic anthropology that scarcity is everywhere present, requiring economizing behavior everywhere. Time, if nothing else, is scarce, and there are other goods and services, such as prestige, that are usually finite. In those societies, economic analysis is appropriate. Opposed to **substantivism,** which represented a long and ultimately unresolved debate in economic anthropology.

Formal-Operational Phase: Age (12 years and on) at which children develop the capacity to think for themselves, and to think of themselves and the world in highly abstract terms.

Frame Substitution: The process whereby the same **form classes** of noun or verb forms are mutually interchangeable.

Fraternal Polyandry: Marriage of one woman to two or more men who are brothers.

Free Goods: In economics, the existence of goods in such plentiful supply that economic analysis is not applicable. Usual examples are air (ignoring air quality) and, at one time, water.

Free Morpheme: A morpheme that can stand alone and have meaning (e.g., *cat*).

Freudian Phases of Personality Development: States of development entail the oral, anal, and Oedipal/Elektra stages. Largely discredited, this model is still used by many anthropologists and psychologists alike.

Freudian Structure of Personality: An attempt to cast behavior in terms of developmental biology, postulates a three-fold personality structure comprising the *id*, or pure psychic energy; the *ego*, which mediates the relationship between desire and reality; and the *superego*, the moral component of the personality.

Fricative: Consonant produced with a constant airflow through the mouth, accompanied by continuous audible noise (f- or s-sound, which are subtypes).

Front: (also known as **Blade**) Part of the tongue just behind the **apex** or tip.

Frontal Bone: Foremost bone of the **cranium.**

Frontal Lobe: Foremost part of the **cerebral cortex** in the brain which deals with purposive behavior and conceptual thought.

G

Gamete: Sex cell, either *sperm* or *ovum.*

Gender: The elaborations and meanings assigned by cultures to the biological differentiations of the sexes.

Gender Differences: Assumed differences between women and men that are attributed to their sex within a given culture.

Gender Division of Labor: The most common division: the assignment of tasks to individuals on the basis of their gender. Except for warfare and public direction (men) and child care (women), there is wide variation as to which task is assigned to which gender.

Gender Roles: Culturally derived expectations that are assigned to men and women on the basis of their sex.

Gender Segregation: Any society in which women and men conduct activities separately; may include residential segregation, as among the Mundurucu of Amazonia or many New Guinea societies.

Gene Flow: The introduction of new genes to an existing population through migration.

Generalized Reciprocity: Altruistic transaction at which gifts are freely given without keeping accounts. This includes pooling of resources within families.

Generational Links: On a kinship chart, ties linking a person of one generation to another person of the next generation.

Generational Terminology: Aunt/uncle terminology in which the same term is applied for all kin of the ascending generation except for sex of aunt versus uncle.

Generative Grammar: Grammar of a specific language whose rules are generated from the **deep structure** of a **universal language.**

Genes: Segments of **chromosomes** or **DNA** that code for specific traits of the organism.

Genetic Causation: The theory that holds that genetic composition determines personality or intelligence, as articulated in such works as *The Bell Curve* by Charles Murray and Richard Herrnstein (1994).

Genetic Drift: Changes in genetic composition—that is, allele frequency—by chance or random factors in small populations.

Genitor: A child's biological father.

Genocide: The deliberate mass murder of one ethnic group by another, often in the name of socioeconomic development or "progress," with the express aim of eliminating that population.

Genotype: The genetic composition of the organism.

Genus: A group of closely related **species.**

Ghosts: Supernatural beings of human origin; many definitions emphasize malevolent qualities, perhaps present because of some unresolved wrong committed against them.

Glide: A synonym of **semivowel.**

Global Level of Integration: The integration of the economic, political, and military forces on a worldwide scale.

Global Production System: An arrangement whereby industries have established *maquiladoras* throughout the world in an effort to capture cheap labor, with parts of the labor process distributed across nations according to cost considerations. Also known as the *international division of labor.* This system has been facilitated by recent innovations in transportation and telecommunications (as you know from using the Internet.)

Global Warming: Also known as the **Greenhouse Effect,** the rise in the average temperature such that glaciers and the polar ice caps are melting, extreme weather is reported around the globe, and Pacific islands are under threat of seawater flooding.

Gloger's Rule: A theory arguing that within the same species, there is a tendency for heavily pigmented populations to be located on the equator (given the length of sunlight) and for lighter pigmented populations to be located away frm the equator.

Glottochronology: A technique of dating divergences in branches of language families.

Gluteus Maximus: Large muscle that attaches the **pelvis** to the **femur;** essential for bipedal gait.

Gods: Supernatural beings, generically, of nonhuman origin.

Grammar: The sum total of all rules of **phonology, morphology,** and **syntax** for any language.

H

Hammerstone: Stone hammer used for knocking **flakes** off a **core.**

Haploid: (adj.) Refers to half the pair in the number of chromosomes of an organism in a **gamete.**

Haptics: Study of social touching.

Hard Hammer Technique: A **flintknapping** technique for making stone tools by striking one stone, or **core,** with another stone, or hammer.

Hard Palate: Roof of the mouth; sometimes also known simply as the **palate.**

Hawaiian System: A mode of kinship reckoning in which all relatives of the same sex and generation are referred to by the same term; aunts are merged terminologically with (assigned the same terms as) mothers, uncles with fathers, and cousins with siblings.

Hemisphere: One of two halves of the brain, with one side of the brain controlling the opposite side of the body. The left hemisphere is concerned with language, whereas the right hemisphere is concerned with spatial abilities.

Heterozygous: (adj.) Having two unlike **alleles** of a particular **gene.**

Historical Linguistics: The study in the changes and divergences of language over time.

Holism: A fundamental principle in anthropology that aspects of any culture must be viewed in the broadest possible context to understand their interconnections and interdependence. All aspects of a culture are considered, together with their mutual fit.

Hominidae: A **family** that comprises the **genera** Australopithecus, **Paranthropus,** and **Homo.** Characterized by **bipedalism,** progressively reduced **dentition,** progressively larger and more complex brains, and the capability of fine manipulation with hands.

Hominoids: A **superfamily** comprising apes and humans. Characterized by relative large and complex brains, absence of a tail, and relatively complex social behavior. See text.

Homo: Genus characterized by bipedalism, large and complex brains compared to *Australopithecus*, and confirmed ability to make and use tools. See text for other attributes.

Homo erectus: First known **Homo** species to use fire and to make relatively sophisticated stone tools, including the **Acheulean tradition** in Africa and Europe, but not in Asia. See text and **Movius Line.**

Homo habilis: First known **Homo** species with confirmed ability to make and use stone tools, these of the **Oldowan tradition.** See text.

Homo heidelbergensis: Also known as "archaic" *Homo sapiens;* fossil specimens vary widely in apelike characteristics around skull, such as **prognathism.** See text for other attributes.

Homo neanderthalensis: Form of **Homo** with features more robust than **Homo sapiens, with whom** lumpers would place in the same species. Associated with **Mousterian tradition.**

Homo sapiens: Modern humans with regional variations in **breeding populations.** Fully bipedal, lacks **prognathism,** pronounced **supraorbital torus,** and **postorbital constriction,** and has most complex brain of all hominid forms. See text for details.

Homosexual Household and/or *Family:* Household comprising a homosexual couple's household or family and their children.

Homozygous: (adj) Having two like **alleles** of a particular **gene.**

Honesty: The rule whereby a researcher must be prepared to accept the outcome of the test or assessment, whatever that may be.

Horticulture: Agriculture based on hand tools, such as the hoe or digging stick.

Hostile Symbiosis: The mutual dependence of two or more parties who are in conflict with each other.

Household (Domestic Group): That part of a family that shares a common residence; families and households may be one and the same or they may not be. Households are classified by family type; thus, **Nuclear Family Household, Extended Family Household,** and so on.

Hylobatidae: A *family* that comprises the lesser apes, the gibbons and the siamangs. Includes specialized **brachiation.**

Hyoid Bone: A bone that anchors the tongue; an important indicator of the presence or absence of language among fossil hominids.

Hypoglossal Nerve: The nerve that runs from the brain directly to the tongue; important for speech articulation. The human hypoglossal nerve is three times the thickness of the chimpanzee's hypoglossal nerve and contains more nerve endings.

Hypothesis: A proposition set forth to be tested. Often referred to as "an educated guess."

I

Iconic: (adj.) Term referring to any expression that cannot be separated from its meaning or context.

Ideal types: A deliberately simplified and abstract representation of a society or its parts to demonstrate how that society or its parts work.

Ilium: Upper blade of the **pelvis.**

Image of Limited Good: Beliefs attributed to peasant or other "traditional" societies that desirable qualities exist only in fixed amounts incapable of increase. Represents a variation of the zero-sum game which one person's gain is another person's loss.

Imperialism: Policies of dominant nation states to gain indirect control of the economy of another nation state or by direct territorial acquisition.

Inbreeding Explanation: The explanation that the **incest tabu** arises from the fear of anomalous characteristics that inbreeding would produce.

Incest Tabu: The prohibition of sexual intercourse between consanguineal kin. Not to be confused with **exogamy,** which emphasizes marriage rather than sexual intercourse.

Incisors: Four front teeth on each jaw which perform cutting functions.

Incomplete Food Production: Food production in which primary reliance is on animal but not plant domestication.

Independence Training: Child-rearing practices that promote independence, self-reliance, and personal achievement on the part of the child.

Infix: An **affix** that occurs within a root or base.

Informant: Persons providing information about their culture or (in linguistics) about their language.

Infraorder: A subcategory of **suborder** that includes Old World monkeys, apes, and humans.

Intensive Cultivation: Cultivation involving high crop yield, usually based on technology ranging from the horse and plow and irrigation to fuel-powered farm machinery such as tractors and threshers. Other definitions include that by Melvin and Carol Ember: "food production that is characterized by the permanent cultivation of fields."

Intensive Horticulture: A variant of high-yield **horticulture** and **intensive cultivation** whereby most or all cultivation is done by hand. **Terrace** cultivation in much of East and Southeast Asia is an example.

Interchangeability: The quality of the communication system such that it can be used by both sender (speaker) and receiver (listener) to send and receive messages.

Intermediate Lineage: Any of a number of lineages embracing **minimal lineages** but also forming a part of larger lineages to the **maximal** lineage.

Interviews: Research that involves asking *informants* questions about their culture, or asking why people do what they do.

Involuntary Recruitment: Rule whereby one is forced to join an organization, such as the military through the draft.

Iroquois System: A mode of kinship reckoning in which father's sister is distinguished from mother and mother's sister, mother's brother is distinguished from father and father's brother, and cross-cousins are distinguished from brothers and sisters and parallel cousins. Parents are classified with the same-sex aunts or uncles, and parallel cousins are classified with brothers and sisters. The Yanomamö reckon their kin by this system.

Irrigation: Any technique of watering crops by diverting water from its source to the fields.

Ischium: Lower bone of the *pelvis* toward the back.

J

Jajmani: An **ascribed** relationship in which a *jajman* provides a good or service to his *kamin* or client; the jajman is born into his occupation and his kamin is his client by birth.

Jati: Any of hundreds of occupational subcastes in India.

Jen: The psychological interface in the human personality between internal psychobiological processes and external social ones, which form the personage of each individual, as suggested by Hsu.

Jihad: Although popular conception regards it a call to struggle against the "infidels," its more basic meaning is the struggle against oneself in one's belief.

Joint (Collateral) Family: One consisting of siblings, their spouses, and their children.

Joint Property: Property owned by a **descent group** or **corporate kin group,** and often referred to as an **estate.**

K

Karma: In Hinduism and Buddhism, the belief that all present lives are the consequences of good deeds and ill of past lives.

Key Informant: Person upon whom the ethnographer primarily or initially depends for information regarding a culture; often selected for extensive knowledge or important local interpersonal connections.

Kindred: Close kin, either bilaterally or unilaterally reckoned, on whom a given ego (from Latin for "I") can call for assistance or to whom he (she) has other types of kinship orientation. Does not involve descent to an ancestor. Except for full siblings (with same mother and father), the kindred differs for each individual, so that kindreds overlap.

Kinesics: The study and analysis of postures, facial expressions, gestures, and body motions that convey meaning, apart from language.

Kingdom: The largest division in the taxonomy of living forms. They include *Plantae* (plants) and *Animalia* (animals), along with three other kingdoms.

Kinship Terminology: See under **Chapter 10.**

Kshatriya: The warrior **caste** in India that includes soldiers and other military personnel, coupled with police and its equivalent.

L

Labio-Labial Stop: Stop formed by closure between upper and lower lips; short term is **bilabial stop.**

Labium: Lip, both upper and lower.

Language Acquisition: Learning a language from infancy to early childhood.

Language Family: A group of languages that are ultimately descended from a single ancestral family (usually reconstructed from this group of languages).

Larynx: Voice box in trachea (the main breathing tube in throat) containing vocal cords, which vibrate when voiced utterances are made. The larynx in humans is located in a lower position on the respiratory tract than those of chimpanzees or other nonhuman vertebrates.

Lateral: Sound made with the sides of the tongue lowered (e.g., l-sound).

Laterite: Oxides of minerals in exposed tropical soil, rendering the soil unsuitable for cultivation. The process of conversion to oxides is known as *laterization.*

Law: Rules that prescribe individual behavior and means of social control ranging from informal sanctions ("customary") to formal, codified rules of conduct and remedies for violation of such rules. Includes mechanisms for conflict resolution.

Left Hemisphere: Left half of **cerebrum** which controls the right side of the body and also deals more extensively with language production and reception than does the right hemisphere.

Legitimacy (in marriage): Social recognition of offspring of a sexual union so that such offspring has full birthrights status in the culture and social status to which they belong.

Legitimacy (In political science and political anthropology)**:** The justification cited for a given political structure, for the right to rule, and the limitations of the exercise of political power.

Leopard Skin Chiefs: Among the pastoral Nuer of Ethiopia and the Sudan, a mediator charged with the task of resolving conflict between two or more parties (families, lineages). They lack the power to force an agreement between the parties and the power to enforce any agreements that are made.

Levalloisian Tradition: A technique for manufacturing large, thin flakes from a carefully prepared core, first created during the Lower Paleolithic, becoming widespread during the Middle Paleolithic.

Levirate: A marriage practice in which a widow marries a brother of her deceased husband (a man, therefore, marries his deceased brother's widow).

Lexemes: Content of a language, sometimes referred to as its vocabulary.

Lexicon: The entire vocabulary of any language.

Liebig's Law of the Minimum: Related to **carrying capacity,** the statement predicts that population cannot grow beyond the limits of a critical resource in an environment, however plentiful other resources may be. Water in a desert environment is an example.

Limbic System: Part of the brain that is involved with several basic bodily functions plus such impulses as sexual desire and self-protection through flight or fight.

Lineages: Unilineal descent groups whose members trace descent through known links **(demonstrate)** from the male or female line to a common ancestor.

Lineal Kin: Kin related in a single line, such as grandfather-father-son (patrilineal in this instance).

Lineal Terminology: Aunt/uncle terminology which separates the parents from the aunts and uncles.

Linguistic Divergence: The development of different languages from an ancestral language.

Linguistic Relativity: The proposition that diverse interpretations of reality embodied in language yield demonstrable influences on thought.

Linguistics: The comparative study of language, primarily as it is spoken.

Local-Genealogical Segmentation: A characteristic of **segmentary lineages** in which closer lineages also dwell more closely with each other, serving as a physical reminder of their genealogy.

Localocentrism: An excessive focus among social researchers on local communities with little attention devoted to socioeconomic forces that originate outside a given community but encroach upon that community.

Logic: The rule whereby a proposition must be both *sound,* that is, be truthful, and *valid,* that is, be based on solid reasoning. A statement can be sound but invalid or be unsound but valid.

Longhouses (Iroquois): Houses in which female members of matrilineages and matrilineal clans form the core residents; consanguineal and affinal males are considered "guests."

Lower Lip: The frontmost of the **Articulators.**

Lumbar Vertebrae: Segmented bones of the lower *vertebrae;* often associated with back pain among human bipeds.

Lumpers: Taxonomists who would make broader distinctions between *taxa;* for example, lumpers would place humans and Neanderthals into one *species.*

M

Magic: The manipulation of supernatural beings and objects.

Male Expendability Explanation: An explanation for the **gender division of labor** in that men handle dangerous tasks inasmuch as if many men lose their lives to hunting, quarrying, or warfare, reproduction need not suffer so long as most fertile women have sexual access to men.

Mammalia: Animals with internal body temperature regulation, usually with hair or fur, and whose females secrete milk. Humans belong to that *class.*

Mana: Forces which are inanimate, that is, have no personality. Derived from the Polynesian, which entails the tabu of objects that have too much force (mana) for commoners to handle. May be compared with electricity, which is invisible but dangerous to those untrained to handle it.

Mandible: Lower jaw.

Maquiladoras: Following the name given to factories in Mexico established near the U.S. border, any plant that performs part of the productive process for **transnational corporations** within the context of a **global production system.** They do not necessarily have to be located near the borders of developed countries.

Marginal Environments: Environments considered too arid, frozen, or moist for **intensive cultivation.**

Market Exchange: Exchange of goods or services, either directly (barter) or indirectly with money (prices), by laws of supply and demand. Classic example: Regional markets in Guatemala, Mexico, and other highland Latin American Indian peasants.

Marriage (Composite of Today's Definitions): A union between two persons sanctioned by society that involves culturally approved sexual activity and often involves economic cooperation.

Marriage (Notes and Queries): "A union between a man and a woman such that the children born of the woman are recognized legitimate offspring of both parents." (Notes and Queries, Royal Anthropological Institute) There are numerous other definitions of the concept.

Marriage Types also serve to classify family types: **Polygynous Family, Polyandrous Family,** and **Nuclear Family.**

Matrifocal Families: One made up of a woman and her children; the father is absent.

Matrilateral Cross-Cousin: Ego's mother's brother's child.

Matrilateral Cross-Cousin Marriage: Marriage of a man to his mother's brother's daughter.

Matrilateral Parallel Cousin: Ego's mother's sister's child.

Matrilineages: Those lineages based on matrilineal descent.

Matrilineal Clans or *Sibs (Matriclans, Matrisibs):* Those clans or sibs organized matrilineally.

Matrilineal Descent: Rule of affiliation with a group of kin through descent links of females only.

Matrilocal Residence: One in which the couple lives with or near the wife's kin (also known as *Uxorilocal Residence*).

Matri-Patrilocal Residence (usual meaning): One in which the husband and wife live with the wife's kin, then later shifts to the husband's kin. Usually occurs where **bride labor** is practiced.

Mauss's Theory of Exchange Obligations: *Obligation to give:* in order to extend social ties to other groups; *obligation to receive:* inasmuch refusal represents a rejection of offer of friendship as well; and *obligation to repay:* inasmuch as failure to do so places receiver in status of beggar to the giver.

Maxilla: Upper jaw.

Maximal Lineage: The largest **lineage** in a society, which usually comprises smaller lineages.

Mediation: The means of resolving conflict through **negotiation,** involving a neutral third party, of which a **leopard skin chief** is an example.

Medical Anthropology: A discipline combining physical and cultural anthropology that applies findings about folk medical beliefs to actual treatment, including such areas as biomedicine, ethnomedicine, and alternative systems of medical care.

Meiosis: Division of a gamete into two, each one containing half the chromosomes of somatic cells.

Men's Houses: In most New Guinea societies, men live together in a common dwelling, handling all the warrior arts, hunting, the dances, and more mundane tasks, such as house repair, clearing gardens, and negotiating pig transactions. Boys move in men's houses at age five or six. Institutionalized homosexuality is often attributed to cohabitation in such residences.

Mercantilism: Policies of dominant nation states that include direct administrative and monopolistic control over the economy of another state, usually its colony.

Merging: Terminological categorization of relatives on the father's side with those on the mother's side.

Metatarsals: Foot bones.

Minimal Lineage: The smallest **lineage** in a society with larger lineages or **clans.**

Minimal Pair: Any pair of forms (roughly, words) identical except for one **phone** found in the same position within an otherwise identical **environment** (e.g., [bIn] and [pIn] are minimal pairs in English. A minimal pair isolates two **phonemes** because [b] and [p] sound different, therefore are significant and make a difference in the meaning of the two utterances).

Mitosis: Division of one *somatic cell* into two.

Modal Personality: The statistically dominant personality type in a given culture. Expressed in statistical terms, the central tendency of a defined frequency distribution of one personality type or another within a culture.

Modernization: The process of cultural and socioeconomic change whereby developing cultures adopt attributes of Western culture (from Haviland 2002:440).

Moiety: One of a set of two related maximal unilineal descent groups or units in a social unit (band, village, or other such unit). Derived from the French meaning "half."

Molars: Three back teeth behind the **premolars,** which perform grinding functions.

Money: Any object used to make payment for goods and services. May also be used to measure value of goods and services and as a store for wealth. Often, the material used in the object may lack intrinsic value. Shells in many societies are one example; paper money is an example in Western countries.

Monogamy: Marriage of one man to one woman.

Monotheism: Belief in one god only.

Morpheme: The smallest unit of meaning in a language. Morphemes may be free (capable of standing alone) or bound (lacking meaning apart from another morpheme). Thus, the expression *cats* is made up of two morphemes: *cat,* which is a free morpheme, and *-s,* which is a bound morpheme.

Morphology: Study of morphemes and their combinations; in reality there is no hard and fast distinction between morphology and syntax.

Mousterian Tradition: A term describing the stone tool assemblages (including notches, burins, denticulate tools, and scrapers) of **Homo neanderthalensis.**

Movius Line: An imaginary line drawn through Central India, east of which no **Acheulean** handaxes have been found. Named after the archaeologist Hallam Movius, who first described this anomaly.

Multinational Corporations: Corporations with operations in two or more nation states.

Multiregional or **Continuity Model:** The theory that modern **Homo sapiens** evolved from earlier hominid populations (**Homo erectus, Homo heidelbergensis,** and **Homo neanderthalensis**) throughout the Old World—Africa, Asia, and Europe—at roughly the same time.

Mutation: An alteration in the genetic material.

N

Nasal Bones: Bones on the face that support the nose.

Nasal Cavity: The cavity behind the nose, often used in speech.

Nasals: Any sound resonating in the nasal cavity. Produced by lowering the **velum.**

Nation: Usually geographically contiguous populations sharing a single ethnicity and language; they include stateless nations, such as the Kurds in Turkey, Syria, Iraq, and Iran. Nations without territories are known as *diasporas*.

Nation State: A nation that is governed by its own *state*, rather than the state of another ethnic group or *nation*. Nations without territories are known as *diasporas*.

National Character: Basic personality traits attributed to citizens of a nation.

Natural Habitat Hypothesis: A hypothesis proposing that agriculture emerged where domesticated plants developed at the site of their natural ancestors.

Natural Selection: Genetic change in the frequency of certain traits in breeding populations because of differential reproductive success between individuals.

Need for Achievement (n-ach): Postulated by McClelland, the notion that "traditional" societies whose members show a drive for accomplishment are the best candidates for development aid. McClelland posits a number of indicators for this "need for achievement" (*n*-achievement or *n*-ach), such as folk tales.

Negative Reciprocity: The attempt to get something for nothing, or for something of lesser value. Ranges from bargaining or haggling to less sociable forms such as theft or other varieties of seizure.

Negative Sanctions: Punishment for noncompliance, ranging from reprimands and fines to imprisonment to the death sentence.

Negotiation: Conflict resolution or agreement through direct talks to reach a compromise or a mutually satisfactory agreement.

Neolithic Revolution: The domestication of plants, animals or both, which first took place about 10,000 years ago.

Neolocal Residence: One established by the couple anew, separately from the kin of either groom or bride.

Nirvana: The realization that this world is illusion and the discovery of the reality beyond this illusory world.

Nomadic Pastoralism: The type of **pastoralism** in which entire families seasonally move with their herds.

Nomenclature: Naming system based on taxonomy.

Nonfraternal Polyandry: Marriage of one woman to two or more men who are not brothers.

Nonsense Words: Words whose phonemes can be combined to form new combinations, but which are devoid of content. Sometimes formerly nonsense words do acquire content, such as the expression *blip* ([blɪp]) which lacked meaning until radar was invented.

Nonsororal Polygyny: Marriage of one man to two or more women who are not sisters.

Noumena: Things and events in a world incapable of sensory perception, as opposed to phenomena, or things and events that can be perceived by the senses.

Nuchal Crest: Area around the base (humans) or back (quadrupeds) of the skull to which neck muscles attach.

Nuclear Family: One composed of a man, a woman, and their unmarried children.

Nucleus: The structure inside the cell that contains the **chromosomes.**

O

Oasis Hypothesis: Hypothesis that posits that agriculture emerged where there was water in an increasingly water-scarce environment.

Oath: Act of calling on a deity to bear witness to the truth of what one says in a formal or informal judicial proceeding; the oath in court is a holdover from this practice.

Obligate Bipedalism: Bipedalism is forced by the human skeletal structure, examples are arched feet, bowl-shaped **pelvis,** inward angling of the **femur,** and so on.

Observation: Informed watching of the behavior of people within a culture with the aim not only of describing this detail or that, but asking how it fits in with the rest of the culture. It may involve learning the language, and observing how that language structures the reality experienced by the people being studied.

Occipital Bone: A bone of the **cranium** located in the lower back.

Occipital Condyles: Rounded process on either side of the **foramen magnum** that articulates the skull with the **cervical vertebrae.**

Occipital Lobe: Part of **cerebral cortex** located in the lower back of the brain; responsible for sight.

Oldowan Tradition: The name given to pebble tools and flakes during the beginning of the Lower Paleolithic; derived from the Olduvai Gorge in East Africa where large assemblages of these tools were found.

Omaha System: A mode of kinship reckoning, associated with patrilineal descent, in which a mother's brother and mother's brother's son are called by the same term, a father and father's brother are merged under another term, and a mother and mother's sister are merged into a third. Parallel cousins are equated with brothers and sisters.

Open Systems (Linguistics): Communication systems whose elements can be combined with others to create new meanings.

Open-Class Society: A society in which **social mobility** often occurs.

Open-Ended Interviews: Unstructured interviews, generally without detailed questionnaires.

Oral cavity: Inside space of the mouth between the lips and the throat.

Ordeal: A means used to determine guilt or innocence by submitting the accused to dangerous, painful, or risky tests believed to be under supernatural control.

Order: A subcategory of *class* (or subclass, superorder, or other category, depending on lifeforms and taxonomic scheme) which includes *Primata.*

Ovum (pl. ova): Female sex cell; when fertilized it becomes a *zygote.*

Ozone Depletion: The thinning of the ozone layer, which filters three kinds of ultraviolet radiation, as the result of increased chlorofluorocarbons in the atmosphere.

P

Palate: Roof of the mouth; also known as the **hard palate** or dome.

Paleolithic: The first period of human prehistory beginning 2.5 million years ago with the **Oldowan Tradition** and continuing with the **Acheulean, Levalloisian,** and **Mousterian Traditions** up to the **Upper Paleolithic.** The period ended with the domestication of plants and animals, known as the Neolithic, around 10,000 years ago.

Panidae: In some taxonomies, a *family* that includes chimpanzees, bonobos, and gorillas, but excludes orangutans, who remain the sole members of the family *pongidae.*

Paralanguage: The extralinguistic noises that accompany language, such as laughing or sobbing.

Parallel Cousin: Ego's father's brother or mother's sister's child.

Paranthropus: A "robust" form of *Australopithecus* categories as a separate genus by *splitters* but not by *lumpers.* Males characterized by *sagittal crest,* and are larger boned compared to the so-called gracile Australopithecines, but are not larger in body size. Include *Paranthropus robustus* and *Paranthropus boisei.*

Parietal Bone: Top and upper side and back bone of the *cranium.*

Parietal Lobe: Top and upper side and back of the *cerebral cortex* which receives sensory information from the body.

Participant Observation: Observation that involves taking part in the activities of the people under study, and describing the experience of this participation.

Pastoralism: Subsistence based exclusively or primarily on the domestication of herding animals, such as cattle, horses, or sheep. Usually found in semi-arid grasslands.

Patella: Kneecap.

Pater: A child's social father. Although usually the **genitor** and **pater** are one and the same man, in **matrilineal** societies, the pater may be the child's mother's brother.

Patrifocal Families: One made up of a man and his children; the mother is absent.

Patrilateral Cross-Cousin: Ego's father's sister's child.

Patrilateral Cross-Cousin Marriage: Marriage of a man to his father's sister's daughter.

Patrilateral Parallel Cousin Marriage: Marriage of a man to his father's brother's daughter, designed to keep the assets, such as sheep or horses, within the lineage; frequently practiced in the Middle East.

Patrilineages: Those lineages based on patrilineal descent.

Patrilineal Descent: Rule of affiliation with a group of kin through descent links of males only.

Patrilineal Clans or *Sibs (Patricians, Patrisibs):* Those clans or sibs organized patrilineally.

Patrilocal Residence: One in which the couple lives with or near the husband's kin (also known as *Virilocal Residence*).

Pattern Variables: From sociology, the notion that indices can measure extremes between "traditional" and "modern" society. Examples: ascription (being born into a task, such as an occupational caste in India) versus achievement (acquiring a position by training and demonstrated accomplishments); particularlism (gaining a position by personal contact: "who you know") versus universalism (gaining a position by meeting requirements by criteria applicable to all: "what you know").

Peak Oil: The point in the cycle of oil production and use where oil ceases to be cheap and plentiful and begins to be irreversibly more expensive and scarce. China's and India's recently increased demand for oil is exacerbating the shortage.

Peasant: A primary producer, usually an agrarian, who is subjected via asymmetrical ties to a state which exercises domain over his assets for which, according to Eric Wolf (1966), he must provide for a fund of rent. Most definitions emphasize linkages between local and supralocal society, usually a state, as reflected in Kroeber's seminal definition of peasants as "part societies with part cultures."

Peasantization (also known as de-agrarianization): The process of cultural change whereby former independent horticulturalists are forcibly linked to the state through taxation, marketization, or other means.

Pelvis: Hipbone composed of *pubis, ischium,* and *ilium,* plus the fused *sacrum* and *coccyx* in the lower *vertebrae*.

Perception: Sensory input through vision, hearing, touch, smell, and taste.

Percussion Flaking: A technique for producing stone artifacts by striking or knapping *crystalline stone* with a hard or soft hammer.

Peripheral Countries: Countries that rely on a single resource for export; at one time, the country was identified with its leading export: Guatemala (coffee), Chile (copper), Argentina (beef and grains), Bolivia (tin), and Zambia (copper) are among the classic examples.

Personality: The distinctive way a person thinks, feels, and behaves. The components include *perception*, or how one perceives reality through the five senses; *cognition*, or how one interprets this reality; *emotion*, or how one feels or thinks about that reality; and *behavior*, or how one responds to that reality.

Personality Formation: Child-rearing practices that foster compliance to the performance of assigned tasks and dependence on the domestic group, rather than reliance on oneself.

Phalanges: Digits (fingers) on the hands and digits (toes) on the feet.

Phenetic Taxonomy: Taxonomy based on physical and adaptive traits of a lifeform.

Phenotype: The observable and measurable characteristics of an organism.

Phone: Any speech sound in a language. Includes clicks and tone of voice.

Phoneme: As used here, the smallest significant unit of speech in a language. It may consist of one phone or more than one similar phones. A phone affects meaning in an utterance (and so is significant) but is not meaningful in itself. Two phonemes sound different to the speakers of the same language (e.g., the two stops in "pin" and "bin" in English.) What matters, therefore, is the contrast between two phones or two clusters of phones.

Phonetics: Study of production, transmission, and reception of **phones,** speech sounds.

Phonology: Study of **phonemes.**

Phratry: Group of supposedly related clans or sibs (other than moieties). Several definitions have been proffered.

Phylum: A subcategory of **kingdom** that includes **Chordata** or animals with spinal cords.

Physical Anthropology: The comparative study of the biological aspects of humankind of both contemporary population and fossil forms.

Plantae: Lifeforms of a **kingdom** that produce their own food by photosynthesis and are incapable of movement, or sessile.

Points of Articulation: Parts in the upper part of the mouth involved in articulation, or forming of speech sounds. These include the upper lip (the only movable part), upper teeth, gum or alveolar ridge, hard palate, and soft palate or velum. See diagram.

Political Anthropology: The cross-cultural comparative study of social control, whether informal or formal; includes political organization, formal or not, and law, formal or customary.

Polyandry: Marriage of one woman to two or more men.

Polygamy: Plural marriage; marriage to more than one spouse (male or female) at the same time.

Polygynandry: Marriage in which two or more men marry two or more women at the same time. Also known as **group marriage;** this practice is extremely rare.

Polygyny: Marriage of one man to more than one woman at the same time.

Polytheism: Belief in multiple gods, often specializing in different realms of human existence.

Polytypic: (adj.) Refers to species composed of populations that differ with regard to one or more traits.

Pongidae: A **family** that comprises the great apes: chimpanzees, bonobos, gorillas, and orangutans. Some taxonomies include orangutans only, whereas the others are classified as **Panidae.**

Population Growth: The exponential growth in world population from 1 billion in 1850, to 6 billion as of the year 2000 with projected growth to be 10.5 billion by 2050.

Population Replacement: An equilibrium between birth and death rates such that populations neither increase nor decrease. China's one-child policy is an attempt to achieve this goal.

Poro Secret Societies: Secret societies in West Africa Mande-speaking peoples in which all men were **involuntarily recruited** for sacred and secular functions in each **chiefdom** of that linguistic group.

Positions of Articulation: The positioning of articulators relative to points of articulation to form a given sound of speech.

Positive Sanctions: Rewards for compliance, such as recognition or monetary rewards.

Postcranial Skeleton: The skeleton below the skull (in humans) or behind the skull (in **quadrupedal** animals).

Potlatch: A feast among most Northwest Coast Indians held to observe a major event, such as the installation of a new chief.

Power: In asymmetrical political relations, the process of securing compliance by force. Classic examples: concentration camps in Nazi Germany or the Soviet Union or the so-called supermax prisons in the United States, such as the Pelican Bay correctional facility in California. Some anthropologists would see this as the defining characteristic of *social control,* or control over groups through overt coercion.

Power Grip: Grip whereby an individual grasps an object between the palm and the fingers; all primates have this ability.

Precision Grip: Grip whereby an individual holds an object, for example a pen, between the thumb and forefingers, thanks to the opposable thumb.

Prefix: An **affix** that is attached to the front of a root or **base** (e.g., *pre-* in *prehistoric*).

Premolars: Two back teeth behind each **canine tooth;** perform grinding function.

Preoperational Phase: Phase (2–6 years) in which symbols, including language, are first used.

Pressure Flaking: A technique for producing stone artifacts by removing **flakes** from a stone core by pressing with a pointed instrument.

Primary Incest Tabu: The prohibition of sexual intercourse between consanguineal members of the immediate family, namely between mother and son, father and daughter, and brother and sister.

Primary Innovation: The discovery of a new principle or technology.

Primary Sex Characteristics: Reproductive systems of the two sexes: the penis, testicles, and associated genital parts of men; and the vagina, fallopian tubes, and uterus of women.

Primata: Animals with stereoscopic vision, opposable thumbs, relatively large brains, and complex social behaviors and relations. See text for further discussion. Humans belong to that **order.**

Pristine States: **States** that theoretically arise in the absence of other states.

Private Property: Property owned by an individual or individuals. Tenure is often called fee simple.

Productivity: The property of communication elements such that they can be combined to form new elements which neither the sender (speaker) nor receiver (listener) has heard/seen before, and yet both understand perfectly.

Proletarianization: The process of cultural change whereby former independent horticulturalists or peasants lose their land or other resources and become dependent on the labor market.

Property: An asset that is owned by some entity—community, kin group, individual—as observed by members of a culture.

Proposition: A statement positing a relationship between two or more things and events. That cultures universally prohibit incest is an example of a proposition (a rather broad one).

Proxemics: The study of personal space.

Pseudoscience: Any belief system making claims to science but lacking scientific *methodology.*

Pubis: Lower front bone of the *pelvis.*

Q

Quadrupedalism: The ability to walk on four feet.

R

Race: Polytypic variation within a human population that is often based on *folk taxonomy.*

Racial Discrimination: The differentiation of groups by physical characteristics and the discrimination exercised against those of the less-powerful group. They include blacks in U.S. society and in apartheid South Africa.

Racism: A *folk taxonomy* that links behavioral attributes, such as intelligence, to *polytypic* differences in human populations.

Radius: Lower arm, which is located thumb side and moves around the *ulna.*

Raid: A short-term use of physical force that is planned and organized to achieve a limited objective, such as cattle or horse theft.

Ranked Societies: Societies in which there are fewer valued status positions than there are persons capable of filling them (Fried 1967).

Recessive (Genetics): (adj.) The situation in which, in a **heterozygous** individual, the gene is not expressed in the phenotype; the trait becomes phenotypic only if the individual is **homozygous** for that trait.

Reciprocity: Direct exchange of goods and services.

Reckoning (of Kin): Selective recognition of (usually) biological kin as members of one's own family or other kinship unit (however, nonkin can be "adopted" and so also "reckoned" as kin, such as godparenthood in Latin countries and adoption in Polynesia).

Redistribution: The means by which goods and services (or claims thereof, such as money) are collected by some central agency (chief, monarch, or modern government) and redistributed in the form of some benefit(s) to the people at large. Classic example: Potlatch and other feasts among Northwest Coast Peoples, such as the Nootka and the Kwakiutl.

Relative Strength Explanation: An explanation for the **gender division of labor** in that men, compared with women, have the strength to carry out more strenuous tasks.

Religion: The supernatural world view that involves recognition of the unseen world and its beings, but does not involve direct manipulation. The emphasis lies on coming to terms with the unseen through supplication to the beings in the form of prayer and ritual. It should be noted that this is not an entirely clear distinction, and some anthropologists would reject this distinction altogether.

Replacement or Out-of-Africa Model: The theory that modern **Homo sapiens** evolved into their present form in Africa, then displaced earlier hominid populations throughout the Old World (Europe and Asia).

Replication: The rule whereby any verified proposition must be subjected to a second test or assessment involving conditions that are identical to the first.

Research Method: The reasoning that leads to the choice among possible research techniques, and the justification for making the choice. Often used interchangeably with **research techniques,** thus creating confusion.

Research Methodology: The principles or research problems that govern the rationale behind a given set of **research methods.**

Research Techniques: Any of several direct ways for gathering information: **observation, participant observation, interview,** technological devices such as videotapes and tape recorders, photographs, written records analysis, and a host of others.

Residence: The household in which a couple resides after marriage. Also known as **postmarital residence.**

Respondent: Person responding to closed-ended interviews; often used in sociology, political science, and other social sciences.

Restitution: The process, whether in customary or formal law, in which a breach is corrected by repaying the injured party for its loss. Restitution is the primary means of conflict resolution in most non-Western societies.

Restricted Ambilineal Descent Group or Restricted Cognatic Descent Group: Bilateral descent groups in which a restrictive rule determines one's membership; an example is the landowning *kainga* among the Gilbertese.

Restudy: Research conducted of a culture previously studied, usually by another anthropologist; the rough anthropological equivalent to **replication.**

Retouching: The shaping or sharpening of a stone artifact through **percussion** or **pressure flaking.**

Retribution: The process, whether in customary or formal law, in which a breach is corrected through punitive means. Retribution is the primary means of conflict resolution in state societies, but it can manifest itself in non-Western societies through blood revenge.

Reverse Dominance: The power a group exercises over an individual who tries to assert power over them; means range from ridicule to homicide.

Revitalization Movements: Movements involving the supernatural that arise when cultures are undergoing a rapid change. Examples: the cargo cults of New Guinea, the ghost dance of the Lakota Indians in the nineteenth century, and even the movement of the Branch Davidians in the early 1990s.

Right Hemisphere: Right half of **cerebrum** which controls the left side of the body and is also involved with spatial abilities.

Rites of Passage: Rituals marking important phases in the life of an individual, in which he or she ritually leaves one status (usually childhood) and enters another (adulthood).

Ritual Apology: A formal apology by the offender to the victim; often accompanied by a reparation gift of value, such as cattle.

Rivalry Potlatches: **Potlatches** characterized by competitive gift giving by rival pretenders to a chieftainship.

Rotating Markets: Markets that change location, usually from day to day during a week.

Rules of Descent (Descent): Rules that connect individuals with particular sets of kin because of presumed known or presumed common ancestry.

Rules of Residence: Applied to extended families, separates family types, so that you can have a ***Patrilocal Extended Family,*** a ***Matrilocal Extended Family,*** and so on.

Rural-to-Urban Migration: A worldwide trend for former agrarian peoples to migrate to the cities as they lose their lands and other resources in rural areas as part of the **proletarianization** process.

S

Sacrum: Fused **vertebrae** forming part of the pelvis.

Sambandham: Among the Nayar, the right of a woman to entertain one of several male partners at night; a child born to the woman was legitimated when one of the men paid delivery costs, a small gift to the midwife.

Samsara: The belief that this world is a cosmic illusion.

Sanctions: Reinforcements for a given rule or law.

Sande Secret Societies: Secret societies in West Africa Mande-speaking peoples in which all women were **involuntarily recruited** for sacred and secular functions in each **chiefdom** of that linguistic group; women often initiated legal proceedings.

Sapif-Whorf Hypothesis: The former name of ***Linguistic Relativity,*** attributed to Edward Sapir and his student, Benjamin Lee Whorf. This is the proposition that diverse interpretations of reality embodied in language yield demonstrable influences on thought.

Scarcity: The notion in economics that goods and services exist in lesser supply than that wanted by humans. The basic postulate is that human wants (needs usually do not enter into the equation) are infinite and that the means for fulfilling them are finite.

Secondary Incest Tabu: The prohibition of sexual intercourse between specified consanguineal kin outside the nuclear family, usually within the same lineage, clans, or other kin-based group.

Secondary Innovation: The application of a new principle or technology to a society or culture, inducing change in that society or culture.

Secondary Sex Characteristics: Derived physical characteristics, such as greater size and wedge-like body structure of men and breasts and wider hips of women.

Secondary States: **States** that arise among, and under the influence of, other states.

Secret Societies: Societies whose secrets are known only to initiates, often associated with supernatural beliefs, such as the Katchina associations among the Hopi of the U.S. Southwest, the ritual societies among the Kwakiutl of the Northwest Coast.

Segment: One of two or more groups whose internal structure (patrilineal, matrilineal, or ambilineal) is similar.

Segmentary Lineages: A social organization based on local lineages unified by an ever-larger set of lineages that are unified by one maximal lineage. Occurrence is rare, and has been described for the Nuer of Ethiopia and the Sudan, the Tiv of Nigeria, and the Rwala Bedouin of the Middle East.

Segmentation or **Fission:** The splitting of a descent unit or group into two or more new descent units or groups. (NOTE: Some intermarrying lineages may divide into smaller intermarrying lineages, as is the case among the Yanomamö).

Self-awareness: The ability to identify oneself as an object, to react to oneself, and to appraise oneself.

Semi-Peripheral Countries: Countries occupying an intermediate position between **core countries** and **peripheral countries,** both in terms of levels of development (some industry is present) and in roles as conduits between the other two types of countries.

Semivowels: Sounds produced with an articulation like a vowel but moving quickly to another articulation (e.g., w-sound, y-sound). Also known as **glides.**

Sensimotor Phase: Phase in which the infant (birth to 2 years) explores the world through touching, sucking, listening, and other sensory modes.

Serial Monogamy: Marriage of one man or woman to several partners over time, but one partner only at a time. Example: Remember Liz Taylor? If not, think tabloid.

Sex: The physical characteristics of men and women.

Sexual Competition Explanation: The explanation that the **incest tabu** arises from the fear that sexual competition among primary kin will disrupt family ties because of jealousy.

Sexual Dimorphism: Physical differences between the sexes. Gibbons lack much sexual dimorphism, inasmuch males and females look very much alike and neither is larger than the other; in contrast, gorilla males are much larger than females; humans fall somewhere in between.

Shaduf: In Egypt, a lever with a bucket that was dipped into the Nile. The water was then transferred to a sluice and thence to the field.

Shaman: Supernatural specialist practitioner who acts as mediator between spirit and material world; often involved with diagnosis, healing, or both.

Sibling Link: On a kinship chart, a tie linking a person to his or her sibling.

Sickle-Cell Anemia: A severe hemoglobin (red blood cellular) disorder that results from inheriting two copies of a mutant allele characterized by red blood cells assuming a sickle shape; such cells block capillaries, resulting in anemia, heart disease, and ultimately, death.

Signal or Sign: Sound or gesture that has a natural, self-evident meaning.

Silent Trade: The exchange of goods and services between partners who are usually in conflict with each other but each of whom has what the other needs or wants.

Simian Shelf: Among early hominids and nonhuman primates, the bone structure in the inside curve of the mandible that reinforces that mandible.

Simple Foraging: Subtype of **foraging** based on low-yield hunting-and gathering technology; often accompanied by nomadism, reliance on sharing.

Slash-and-Burn Cultivation: (also known as *swidden farming*) In which cultivation is accomplished by first clearing a site of brush and trees and, later, by burning the slash and planting the garden amid the ashes.

Slavery: The forced and involuntary servitude of a population, such as blacks in West Africa during the period from the sixteenth to the nineteenth century; there are signs of a resurgence of slavery in the present.

Social Class: A generic term referring to social categories among all societies, from **egalitarian** to **ranked** to **stratified;** they may include subtypes of **gender,** occupation, and social stratum.

Social Mobility: The ability for an individual to move from one social class to another.

Sociocentric Groups: Groups of organizations centered around descent from a common ancestor.

Sociocultural Level of Integration: The levels of organization in cultures from the local (family or **band**) to the **state** to the global levels; some societies end at the band levels; others add additional layers of organizations.

Sociolinguistics: The study of language as related to attributes of society, such as gender differences of expression, social class usage, and others.

Sodalities: Groups that cut across kin-based ties, such as **age grades and age sets** in East Africa, **men's houses** in New Guinea, and **secret societies** in West Africa and indigenous North America.

Soft Hammer Technique: A *flintknapping* technique for making stone tools by striking a stone, or core, using a hammer of antler, wood, or bone rather than stone.

Soft Palate: Synonym of **velum.**

Solar Markets: Markets located at a central location, usually a town or city, within a region.

Somatic Cell: Any cell of the body except the sex cells, or *gametes*.

Sorcery: Supernatural practice manipulating the supernatural with the intent to bring harm to others by ritual means; practitioners are called *sorcerers*.

Sororal Polygyny: Marriage of one man to two or more women who are sisters to each other.

Sororate: A marriage practice in which a widower marries his deceased wife's sister (a woman, therefore, marries her deceased sister's husband).

Sound: (adj.) The norm that a proposition be true.

Specialization: Ability to transmit highly complex messages by relatively short expressions or utterances. Language is the most specialized of all communication systems.

Special-Purpose Money: Money used for exchanging special classes of objects; *kula* valuables (white armshell and red necklace) among the Trobriand Islanders are examples. Tokens for bus transit are another.

Speciation: The process by which new species are developed from earlier ones.

Species: The largest natural population whose members are able to reproduce successfully (i.e., reproduce fertile offspring) but not with members of other species. By that definition, *Homo sapiens* is one species.

Sperm: Male sex cell, which fertilizes the *ovum*.

Spirant: Synonym of **fricative**.

Spirits: Supernatural beings, usually of human and local origin; refer to ancestral spirits who may visit their localities of origin, such as Balinese or of Latin countries during Day of the Dead (November 1).

Splitters: Taxonomists who make relatively fine distinctions between *taxa;* for example, splitters would place modern humans and Neanderthals into two separate *species*.

Stage Theory of Economic Growth: Postulated by Rostow, a fivefold stage theory of economic development from the traditional to the age of high mass consumption.

State: A society with a head or head whose power is derived from the monopoly of the exercise of legitimate force. Derivative institutions include an administrative hierarchy, delegation of force among police and military institutions, and codified law.

State Terrorism: The deliberate use of lethal force by a national government to control or eliminate selected populations within states, such as the *kulaks* (wealthy peasants) in the Soviet Union under Stalin, the Armenian genocide in 1915 Turkey, or the extermination of the Jews under Nazi Germany.

Stipulated Descent: Tracing of descent through assumed, though not known, links to a given ancestor.

Stock: All the descendants of a person or of a married couple.

Stops: Speech sounds formed when an articulator is pressed against a point of articulation to stop air passage momentarily. There are other types as well—laterals and spirants to name two.

Stratified Societies: Ranked societies in which an elite minority controls the strategic resources that sustain life (Fried 1967).

Structural Duality: The quality, distinct in human languages, of two sets of language structure: significant nonmeaningful sounds (**phonemes**) and meaningful arrangements of sounds (**morphemes** and **syntax**).

Structural Violence: Violence generated by economic, political, and social structures and institutions. Classic examples: low wages in the **maquiladoras** in underdeveloped countries that fail to provide the basic necessities for the workers; murders of those involved in movements for social justice, such as the 500,000 known assassinations and "disappearances" during the hidden civil war in Guatemala (1960–1996).

Suborder: A subcategory of **order** which includes **Anthropoidea** and Prosimii, or prosimians, such as the lemurs, tarsiers, and loris.

Subphylum: A subcategory of **phylum** that includes **Vertebrata,** or animals whose spinal cord is protected by a hard segmented column made of bone or cartilage.

Subsistence Systems: Technology of food production together with the influence that it bears on a cultures' social and economic organization.

Substantivism: The perspective in economic anthropology that emphasizes cultural relativism in the cross-cultural study and comparison of (primarily) nonindustrial economies. Among the principles are the nonexistence of **scarcity** in many societies, the inapplicability of Western economic models and analyses to non-Western societies, and the embeddedness of economies in the other institutions of non-Western society. Opposed to **formalism** which emphasizes universal scarcity.

Sudanese System: (also known as **descriptive system**) A mode of kinship reckoning in which a father, father's brother, and mother's brother are distinguished from one another, as are a mother, mother's sister, and father's sister. Cross and parallel cousins are distinguished from each other as well as from siblings.

Sudra: The peasant **caste** in India that includes all menial workers.

Sufficiency: The rule whereby evidence to support the proposition must be adequate with the following stipulations: (a) the burden of proof rests on the author of the proposition; (b) extraordinary propositions require extraordinary evidence; and (c) evidence based on authority or testimony is never adequate.

Suffix: An *affix* that is attached to the end of a root or *base* (e.g., *-s* in *cats*).

Superfamily: A subcategory of *infraorder,* which includes apes and humans. Separates *Hominoidea* (apes and humans) from Cercepithecoidea, or old world monkeys.

Supernatural Beings: Those perceived as supernatural persons, or at least attributed with a personality or personage.

Supply: The willingness and ability to sell a good or service at a given price.

Supraorbital Torus: Brow ridge among humans and other primates.

Surface Structure: Rules governing the grammar of a specific language.

Symbol: Sound or gesture whose meaning is bestowed to a thing or event that intrinsically has nothing to do with that sound or gesture.

Sympathetic Magic: Magic that involves the belief that like produces like: the stereotypical practice of inserting pins into a likeness of the victim is one example. Also known as *imitative magic*.

Syncretism: The combination of two or more supernatural beliefs, such as folk Catholicism in Latin America and the combination of Islamic belief with *jinn* spirits in much of the Middle East.

Syntax: Roughly, rules by which words (more accurately **morphemes**) are arranged to form phrases and sentences.

T

Tarsals: Anklebones.

Taxon (pl. Taxa): Individual category based on a classification system. See **taxonomy.**

Taxonomy: Classification system based on similarities and differences, arranged hierarchically from the general to the specific.

Tay-Sachs Disease: An enzyme deficiency of lipid metabolism inherited through a pair of recessive alleles, causing death in early childhood.

Technology: Tools and other material equipment combined with the knowledge for making and using them.

Temporal Bone: A bone of the *cranium* located on either side of the skull near each ear.

Temporal Lobe: Lobes located at either side near the ears which deal with perception and memory. Auditory cortex handles hearing.

Terraces: Cultivated hillside ridges used to maximize arable land and to capture moisture, often involving **irrigation.**

Territory: The land occupied by a polity (**band, tribe, chiefdom,** or **state**) that is enclosed by boundaries that mark it off from other political entities; they tend to be more clearly defined at the chiefdom and state levels of integration than at the band or even tribal levels of integration.

Theocracies: Governmental bodies consisting of priests or other leaders who derive their power from religion.

Theoretical Orientation: A body of propositions oriented to models that guide research. Examples include culture ecology and functionalism. See under "Anthropological Theory."

Theory: A hypothesis confirmed by laboratory tests, field research, or other means of verification. All theories are *probabilistic:* a theory currently accepted may later be rejected as new evidence becomes available.

Thoracic Vertebrae: *Vertebrae* located in the back of the rib cage.

Tibia: Larger of the two leg bones, located at front.

Tongue: The main **articulators** of the **vocal tract,** divided into the **apex,** the **front** or **blade,** the **centrum** or **body,** and the **dorsum.**

Trade-Related Intellectual Property Rights Agreement (TRIPS): part of the Marrakech Agreement signed off by member nations of the World Trade Organization, is designed to prevent underdeveloped countries from copying or stealing proprietary technology, but also claims proprietary rights over the less developed countries' (LDCs') natural resources.

Trait: The physical characteristics of any organism.

Transhumant Pastoralism: The type of pastoralism based on a pattern of seasonal migration of herds to different environmental zones; usually only men and boys participate, not entire families.

Transnational Corporations: Corporations with highly integrated operations extending throughout two or more nation states.

Tribe: A segmentary society with two or more lineages, clans, or other social groups bound together by marriage, pantribal sodalities, such as age grades and sets, more inclusive lineages or clans, or some other unifying factor.

Tributary Mode of Production: An arrangement whereby an elite extracts goods in kind or labor from **peasants.**

Twin Studies: First initiated at the University of Minnesota. Holds that identical or **monozygotic** twins, but not fraternal (**dizygotic**) twins, who are reared separately, are likely to display similar personality traits.

U

Ulna: The lower arm, which is located on the little finger side that rotates and moves the **radius.**

Unaspirated Utterance: Those without strong expulsion of air.

Unilateral Kindred: A group of kin in which ego reckons only the father's or the mother's retinue of relatives.

Unilineal Descent: Rule of affiliation with a group of kin through descent links of one sex only.

Universal Ascription: Assignment to any category that affects everyone in all cultures, such as age or gender.

Universal Grammar: A common set of structures that underlie all languages, according to the linguist Noam Chomsky.

Universalistic Religions: Religions purporting to represent all humankind: Christianity, Judaism, Islam, and other so-called world religions are examples.

Unrestricted Ambilineal Descent Group or *Unrestricted Cognatic Descent Group:* Bilateral descent group in which all members of the founding ancestor are members; example is the Gilbertese *oo.*

Unvoiced or *Voiceless Utterances:* Those in which vocal cords in the larynx are not vibrating.

Upper Lip: Frontmost of the **points of articulation;** the only one that moves.

Upper Paleolithic: The period in which tool assemblages became more specialized, the stone tools smaller (microliths), and non-stone materials (bone, ivory, wood) also became commonplace.

Upper Teeth: One of the *points of articulation.*

Usufruct: The right to use and enjoy property belonging to another entity.

Uvula: Small, fleshy membranous tissue hanging at the back of the **velum.**

V

Vaishya: The craftsman and merchant **caste** in India.

Validity: (adj.). The norm that one proposition logically follows from another.

Variable Ascription: Assignment of categories found in only some, but not all, cultures, such as ethnic or regional associations.

Varna: One of four "pure" castes in India, namely the *Brahmin* (priests), *Kshatriya,* (warriors), *Vaishyas* (artisans), and *Sudras* (peasants).

Velum: Soft area behind the **palate** or roof of the mouth. Sometimes called the **soft palate.**

Vertebrae: Segmented backbone.

Vertebrata: Animals whose spinal cord is protected by a bony or cartillagenous segmented column. Humans belong to that *subphylum.*

Vicos Project (Cornell-Peru Project): A classical case study in **applied anthropology** of an hacienda that was transformed from a feudal estate to a commercial farm owned and operated by the former peasants. Despite its evident success, the Peruvian government blocked efforts in other peasant communities to emulate the CPP.

Villagization: The process of cultural change whereby formerly nomadic peoples are persuaded or forced to move into villages. Found largely in countries of East Africa, the Middle East, and former Soviet republics, such as Uzbekistan and Kazakhstan.

Vocal Cords: Two cords in **larynx** whose folds, when drawn tight, produce the voice in voiced utterance. More specifically, a set of muscles inside the larynx that may be positioned in various ways to produce a voice or other glottal sounds.

Vocal Qualifiers: Sound productions of brief duration that modify utterances.

Vocal Segregates: Sound productions that are similar to the sounds of language, but do not appear in sequences that can properly be called words. Examples: *oh oh* to indicate apprehension, or *uh* to fill in spaces while the speaker is searching for the right word or phrase.

Vocal Tract: The oral cavity, nasal cavity, and pharynx (which contains the **vocal cords** and the **larynx** that houses them.)

Vocalization: Paralinguistic noises that are turned on or off at perceivable and relatively short intervals.

Voice Characterizers: Sound productions (laughing, sobbing, trembling) that individuals speak through.

Voice Qualities: The background characteristics of a speaker's voice.

Voiced Utterances: Utterances that involve vibration of vocal cords in larynx, or voice box.

Voluntary Recruitment: Rule allowing one to choose to join an association or not.

Vowels: Resonant sounds produced by the shape within the **oral cavity.**

W

War: Armed combat between human groups comprising separate territorial entities or political communities; at the **state level of integration,** war tends to be systematically planned and implemented; it is likely to involve civilians as well as the combatants, and incorporate progressively higher levels of technology.

Wernicke's Area: Area in the **left hemisphere** that is involved with the perception of spoken language.

White Magic: Manipulation of supernatural forces intended to benefit others.

Windigo: Fear among Algonkian Indians of the northeastern United States and eastern Canada that monsters with a craving for human flesh will turn an individual into a cannibal. There is little evidence that cannibalism was practiced among Algonkian peoples.

Witchcraft: Supernatural forces unleashed, according to some definitions, that bring harm to others through attitudes or ill feeling on the part of the perpetrator, or *witch,* rather than performance of actual rituals. (Classic definition: poison oracle among Azande—chicken and strychnine, as reported by Evans-Pritchard). Other definitions equate witchcraft to *sorcery.*

Woman Marriage: The marriage of two women among the East African Nuer and Nandi, among others, to legitimate the property held by a barren woman and to provide offspring by her partner. The barren woman is the "female husband" in this arrangement.

World Systems Analysis: The theory, elaborated from *dependency theory,* which divides the global economy into *core countries* that draw resources and exploit the cheap labor in *peripheral countries* through the conduits that involve *semi-peripheral countries.* Articulated by Immanuel Wallerstein and his associates.

Z

Zygote: Fertilized ovum, which develops into an embryo and fetus through *mitosis.*

KINSHIP DIAGRAMS

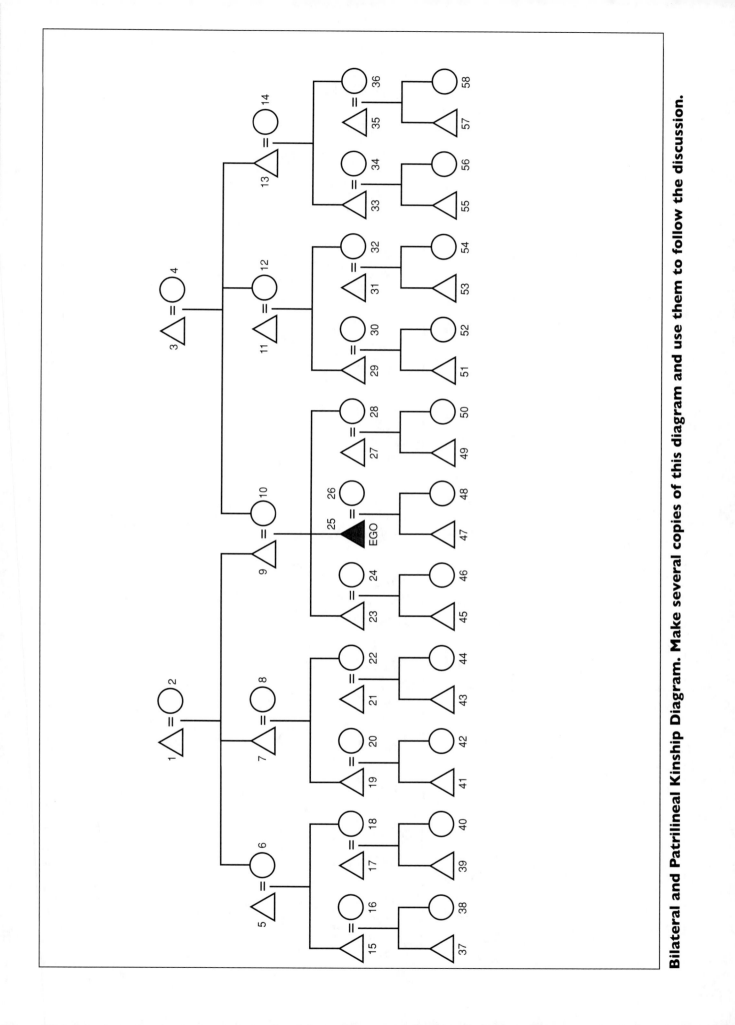

Bilateral and Patrilineal Kinship Diagram. Make several copies of this diagram and use them to follow the discussion.

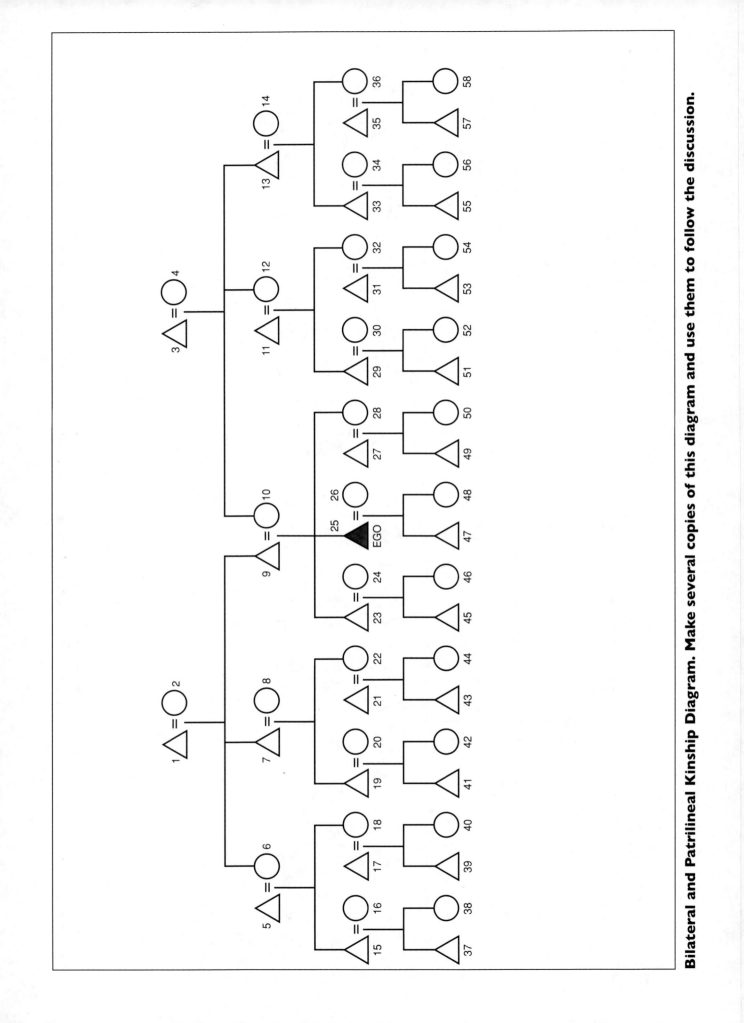

Bilateral and Patrilineal Kinship Diagram. Make several copies of this diagram and use them to follow the discussion.

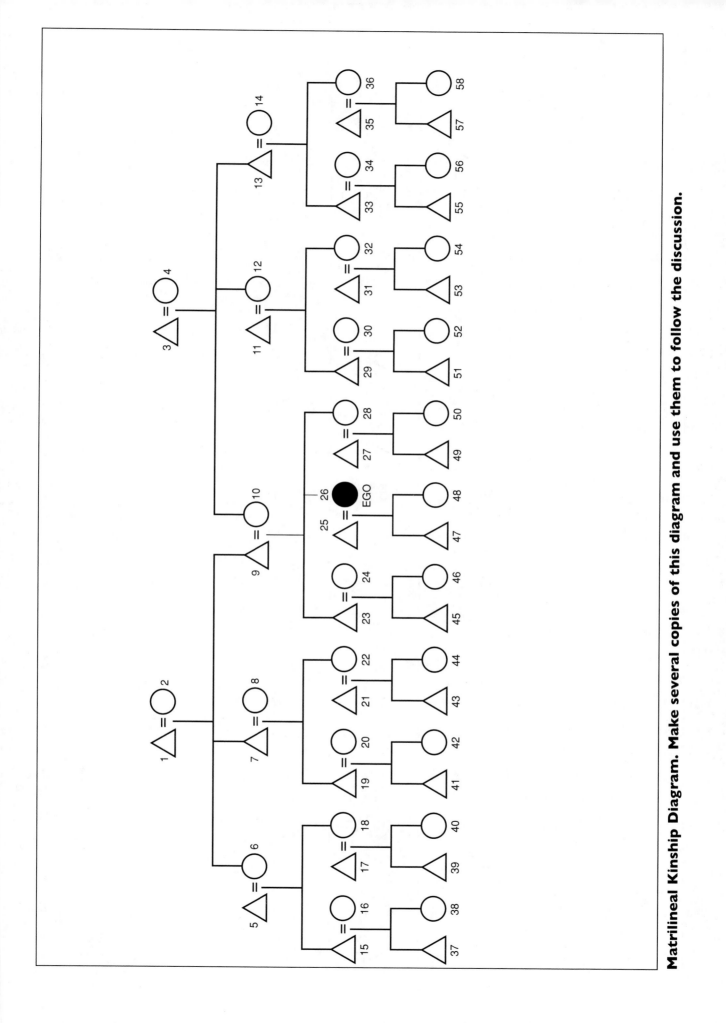

Matrilineal Kinship Diagram. Make several copies of this diagram and use them to follow the discussion.

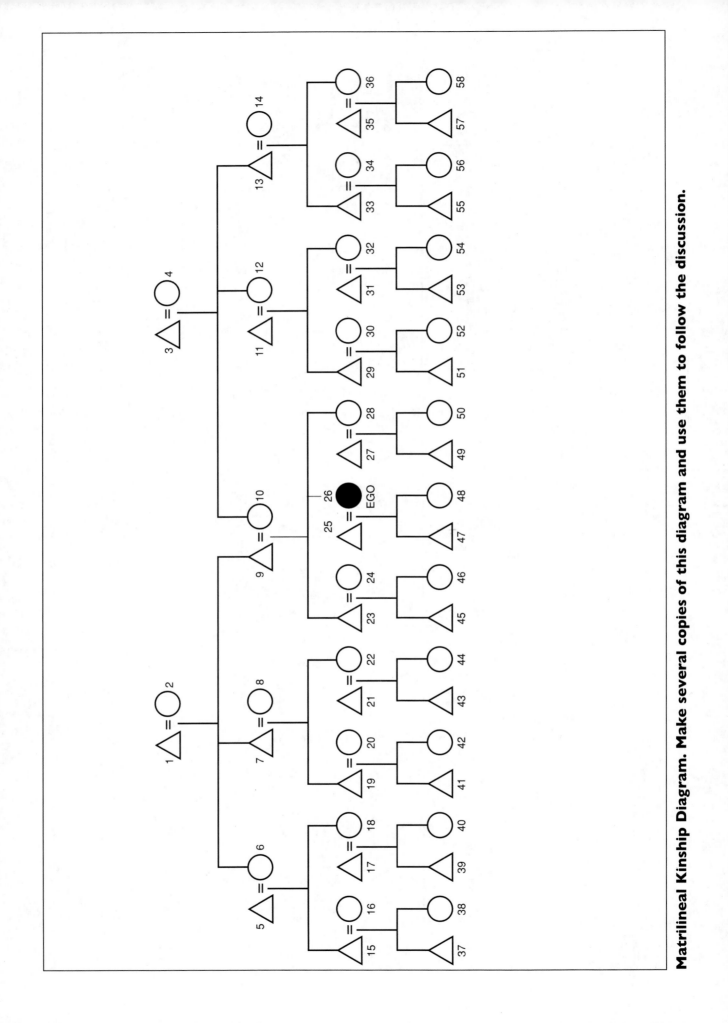

Matrilineal Kinship Diagram. Make several copies of this diagram and use them to follow the discussion.